# Another Way
# of Seeing

# Another Way of Seeing

## Marilyn Baker

**WORD PUBLISHING**

WORD (UK) Ltd
Milton Keynes, England

WORD AUSTRALIA
Kilsyth, Victoria, Australia

WORD COMMUNICATIONS LTD
Vancouver, B.C., Canada

STRUIK CHRISTIAN BOOKS (PTY) LTD
Maitland, South Africa

ALBY COMMERCIAL ENTERPRISES PTE LTD
Balmoral Road, Singapore

CHRISTIAN MARKETING NEW ZEALAND LTD
Havelock North, New Zealand

JENSCO LTD
Hong Kong

SALVATION BOOK CENTRE
Malaysia

ANOTHER WAY OF SEEING

ISBN 0-85009-139-X (Australia 1-86258-048-0)

Typesetting by Suripace Limited, Milton Keynes.
Reproduced, printed and bound in Great Britain for Word (UK) Ltd, by
Cox & Wyman Ltd., Reading, Berkshire

94  95  96  97 / 10  9  8  7  6

## DEDICATION

To my mother and father without whose love, support and encouragement I wouldn't have achieved so much.

## NOTE OF THANKS

Many other people have been a source of inspiration and help in my life. Although I cannot mention you all, I want to say a big thank you for all you have meant to me. You are not forgotten.

# CONTENTS

# One

# Realisation

I had always felt accepted by people so it came as a total surprise when I was nine to realise that some people might think I was different. A customer called at our home one day to see my father, who was the owner of a garage. Dad enthusiastically introduced the gentleman to my mother:

"This is my wife Marion."

"Hello, nice to meet you."

"And this is my daughter Marilyn."

"Lovely to meet ......Oh ......" His voice fizzled out. "I didn't realise ......I am sorry..."

He realised I was blind and started to apologise. Sensing his embarrassment, for the first time in my life I felt ashamed of my blindness. It dawned on me that it was a handicap which not only affected me but could affect my relationships with other people. Up until then it just hadn't occurred to me that anybody might think I was different. My parents had come to terms with my handicap, wanting me to be accepted for myself, and it says a great deal for their handling of the situation that I was nine before I was faced with this realisation.

I had been born in Birmingham into a middle class family. My parents had been married almost ten years and my mother was thirty-eight when I was born a month prematurely. I was fit and healthy, but Mum was ill after a difficult birth so both of us stayed in hospital where I was bottle-fed. During one particular feeding time I choked and that, combined with my being premature, made the nursing staff decide to put me in an oxygen tent for a short while. When Mum got better we went home and there was great excitement amongst family and friends. Nobody knew that anything untoward had occurred.

After about seven months Mum noticed that I had a squint, so she took me to the hospital, where I stayed for a week. It was a shattering blow to my mother when she was told afterwards that I would eventually become completely blind. The same thing was happening to lots of babies at that time, but the reason wasn't known until it was discovered in the early 1950's that they had all been exposed to too much oxygen. My mother had to take me home on the bus and recalls that she cried most of the way. The news was quite unexpected, and a dreadful blow to both my parents. I was their long awaited child, their pride and joy, and to be told that I would one day be totally blind - and for no apparent reason - was devastating.

Gradually over the next year, I lost my sight completely. Neither of my parents had had any dealings with blind children, but they were determined that I would get some enjoyment out of life. Mum was resourceful, and whenever she left me in the pram in the garden, she would always put the radio on so that even though I couldn't see the scenery, I would not feel isolated. Maybe this accounts for my showing a great deal of interest in music at an early age! Apparently I often whistled *Pop goes the Weasel* and other simple tunes.

One day Mum and Dad decided that they would like to have me christened. Although they had not had much to do with church, they felt they would like a special service. They approached the local Bishop, whose comment was, "There are lots of other children being christened and you could bring her too if you'd like". Mum and Dad decided this wasn't appropriate or personal enough and went home disappointed. It was unfortunate that they didn't get the help from the church which they'd hoped for at this point.

My uncle had had quite a lot to do with spiritualist faith healers so he suggested my parents contact Harry Edwards, a well known person in that field. Mr. Edwards wrote to them several times assuring them of his prayers and they sent him money, but I didn't actually meet him. Eventually a local congregational minister, Mr. Cliff, who had done broadcasting on radio and television, performed a lovely and appropriate christening service. He prayed specifically that God would in some real and special way make up to me for my blindness and that I would come to know His love. For my parents this was a memorable occasion.

Mum and Dad were determined that I would get as much out of life as I could. I was quite late learning to walk, but once started there was no stopping me and even though I sometimes hurt myself badly by running into things, they did everything they could to encourage and help me. On one occasion, I came rushing in from outside and hit my head hard on the cooker. This upset them, but of course I soon recovered and became a very hardy toddler. A wooden board was put up to block off the stairs so that I couldn't climb them but, being adventurous, I clambered over it easily. In the end, the bottom board was taken down, but the one at the top stayed to remind me that the stairs were there.

Our home was a spacious detached house, which Dad had had built specially for him and Mum. At the back of the house were some lovely woods and Mum and I spent many happy hours walking and making new discoveries in them.

I had a very happy childhood and grew up enjoying life. Being very inquisitive I wanted to experience as many different things as possible. My parents never showed any sign of awkwardness or resentment about my blindness. As far as I was concerned, life was exciting and full of new adventures. I enjoyed playing games and had a glorious time in our out-house, hammering nails into wood and imagining myself making all sorts of wonderful things. I would run into the house yelling excitedly, "Mum, look at this. What d'you think?" and she was always most appreciative of my creations. One day when I was about three, I gave her a real shock because I told neighbours that I was having a sale and proceeded to offer them bits of wood I'd hammered together with nails into crosses or other simple shapes. I was so proud when I was given a penny or two for them, but I think Mum must have been most embarrassed!

Dad was a very keen fisherman and particularly liked salmon fishing. We had a caravan near Aberdovey and he fished the Dovey river. He would come back with a salmon and encourage me to feel its shape so that I could understand what a fish was like and realise what I was eating later on. Served with parsley sauce and potatoes, freshly caught salmon was my favourite meal.

It took about three hours to get to our caravan, and to me this seemed a never-ending journey. Mum packed sandwiches and, as soon as we left home, I wanted to start on our picnic! 'I spy with my little eye' was a favourite game, and it never occurred to me that I wasn't actually seeing anything! As far as I was concerned 'I spy' meant 'I notice' or 'I am thinking about'. It didn't matter that I couldn't actually see it - I knew what a steering wheel felt like and knowing that there was one in the car I would say, "I spy with my little eye something beginning with 'S'". The journey did seem to pass more quickly when we played this game.

Sometimes relatives came with us to the caravan and we had a wonderful time. Mum didn't like swimming and would not allow me to go paddling in deep water, although we often walked along the beach and she would let me jump into small pools. Sometimes my grandmother enjoyed the walks as well. My Uncle Alan was a good swimmer and often took me into the sea. I would enjoy sitting on a lilo and he would hold me safely while the waves bounced around. But one day I fell off the lilo and it frightened me a great deal. As a result I wasn't quite so adventurous regarding water, much to Mum's relief!

Steam trains ran along the sands at Aberdovey when we first went there. They had a characteristic smell which, although pungent, evokes happy memories even now. The whistle would blow as the train chugged along the side of the beach. Trying to catch it I would run along crying, "Mum, Mum, I'm going to catch the train". Running along the sand was a memorable experience. I felt free and when the wind blew my face and hair it was exhilarating.

A favourite toy of mine down at the caravan was a piece of rubber piping. I would run it along the bottom of the caravan and imagine the different noises of all kinds of things as I sat on the steps making up stories. On one occasion I left this piping behind and was terribly upset - it meant more to me than any other toy or plaything.

Since my father owned a garage, he came home with different cars to try out. It was a great thrill to ride around with him at lunch times and my interest in cars was fostered from an early age. He drove at quite a speed to make it exciting for me and used to tell me about the various types of car, so I soon began to feel an expert. I enjoyed the feeling of movement and in winter Mum took me tobogganing into the woods. She pulled the sledge and would let me go down gentle slopes. It was wonderful. On one occasion though, the sledge hit her ankle and hurt her. She was in agony but, because I didn't understand, I simply laughed - not a very thoughtful thing to do, but I couldn't help myself.

Being an only child and being blind meant that I spent a great deal of time with my mother, so she was also my best friend. We enjoyed doing things together. I also looked upon Nan Lou, my mother's mother, as a confidante and friend. I saw more of her than I did of my other grandmother and was therefore closer to her. At weekends while Mum and Dad went to their club Nan would come to stay and babysit. We shared a double bed and I enjoyed cuddling up beside her. I told her many secrets and knew they were safe with her.

I was an inventive child and my good imagination made up for my lack of sight. I associated smells with certain things: when Mum said she'd been to have her hair permed for instance, this was always accompanied by a burnt smell. I decided that my musical teddy bear would appreciate a perm because although I didn't like the feel of the curls, I knew Mum had it done to make herself look attractive.

"What on earth are you doing, love?" she asked, when I was being busy and secretive.

"Never mind, I'm doing an important job," I replied and proceeded to get the hair-dryer, which as it happened was still plugged in. I achieved the desired smell of a perm by unintentionally burning a patch on the bear's back.

"Mum I've permed teddy's hair. Come and look," I shouted happily. She wasn't very pleased!

When I was about four and a half decisions had to be made about my schooling, so a social worker came to assess whether I would cope with going to a local school for the blind as a weekly boarder. All I knew was that a lady was coming to the house to meet Mum and me and that for some reason this was an important event. Mum kept emphasizing that I was to be on my best behaviour. I wanted to look my best, so went upstairs to get ready. Whenever Mum did this I knew that she put on make-up and did her hair. I wanted to give everybody a surprise and impress the important visitor, so I went into Mum's bedroom and applied lipstick, powder and anything else I could find. The final touch was a set of beads. Mum called up the stairs:

"Marilyn, come along love. The lady is waiting to see you."

"Wait a moment, I'm just getting myself posh," I shouted.

When I got downstairs, my mother gave a sort of shriek, and the social worker burst out laughing. I didn't know what was so funny.

"Oh Marilyn love, where did you get those things?"

"I wanted to make sure I looked really nice," I replied.

The social worker laughed again and even though I must have looked a terrible mess and probably ruined Mum's make-up, neither of them seemed annoyed. The social worker decided that I was quite suitable to go to a school for the blind in Bromsgrove.

# Two

# Boarding School

The big day dawned in September 1955 when I started at Lickey Grange School. Mum and Dad had tried to prepare me for the separation and on the first morning I wasn't too perturbed at leaving them. It was only later, when I realised that I had to stay at school and couldn't see them, that the reality of my new life sank in. At home I had felt secure, but now I was surrounded by the noise of lots of children rushing around. It was a drastic change as I hadn't even been to nursery school or a playgroup. For my parents too this was a very hard time, because we had always been a close-knit family.

I became friendly with another new girl, Maureen Holmes. We both felt the need of a special friend, and stayed close right through primary and junior schools.

Life at boarding school was governed by strict rules which dictated even the way we slept - we had to lie with hands together under our heads. I couldn't sleep like this and sometimes stayed awake for hours because I knew one of the mistresses would check how we were lying. I would wait until she'd been round before getting into my usual curled-up position and dropping off to sleep. I was only five and I missed my mother, especially at night.

School assemblies were something I just did not understand. At home, Mum had read me stories about Jesus and I had enjoyed them very much, but in school although the hymns were about Jesus too, the words were old fashioned and I didn't understand what they meant. It all seemed very strange.

Going to boarding school meant that I learnt to do lots of things for myself. Soon after I arrived, I began to learn braille. Braille is made up like a domino square with six dots, which can be put into different shapes and combinations to make up letters. We had six pins which we stuck into a board and so learnt the alphabet.

Ideas about education in the fifties were very different from what they are now and it was thought better for us to have only limited contact with our parents. We were allowed to see them on Saturdays but not to go home for the whole weekend, even if we lived near enough. I was always heartbroken when I had to return to school. As a result, my parents fought hard, and eventually I was allowed to go home on Saturday mornings, returning to school early on Mondays. This caused a real upset in school, because none of the other parents had this arrangement, but it was worth it as I looked forward to going home all through the week. Eventually, the rules were changed so that children *could* go home at weekends. Sometimes I took with me friends who lived too far away to go to their own homes and we spent some happy days together. So although I hated certain aspects of boarding school, there were good times and I still saw quite a lot of my parents.

Soon after starting school, I began learning to play the piano. Of course I couldn't learn with music because I was only just learning braille, so the teacher played tunes on the piano and I repeated them to her. She also taught me scales. Unfortunately, I found the lessons boring so didn't concentrate at all.

"Now, did we go over this piece last week, Marilyn?" she would enquire.

I often replied that we hadn't even when we had, because then I wouldn't have to learn another new one! It was so much easier to go over the same pieces week after week and she didn't seem to remember what I'd done. Consequently, I didn't get on very quickly with my piano lessons, to the disappointment of my parents.

Mum wanted to be able to communicate with me

without someone else having to read her letters, which inhibited what she wanted to say. So even though she was over forty, she made a real effort to learn braille, reading it with her eyes rather than by feel and writing it with a writing frame. This flat machine sandwiches a piece of paper and enables blind people to punch dots into it uniformly. All the letters have to be written in reverse, so that they can be read when the paper is turned over. It was a complicated task but by learning the alphabet and one or two abbreviations, Mum managed very well and we corresponded in this way. It was so lovely to get personal letters from her in braille because it gave her more freedom in what she wrote.

I loved receiving her letters, but I'm afraid it wasn't until cassettes became popular many years later that I started to communicate back regularly with her.

As a young child I had always enjoyed playing in the garden. Often during lunch times Dad would push me hard on the swing in the outbuilding. I found this exciting and although I was half afraid, I would laugh with delight. I had no thought of selfconsciousness or awkwardness when moving around at home, but at school I began to have problems. I became particularly frightened in PE lessons, especially when climbing onto boxes or jumping off them. The other children seemed much more agile than me and in comparison I felt clumsy. The thrill of heights turned to terror, especially on the climbing frame. Unfortunately the teachers didn't understand this and just told me to try harder - they said I would soon get used to it.

Because the school seemed so huge after the secure environment of home, for the first time I felt generally anxious and unsure of myself. I had difficulty in finding my way around the school buildings and grounds and was often left behind by other girls, arriving late for lessons. Each girl had a set time to practise music and I became afraid of being left in the building at night. I used to hurry my practice time and shout for the other girls to wait for me but very often they didn't. It was great fun to them, but to me it was a nightmare.

It transpired later that the reason for my confusion about direction was that the oxygen given to me as a baby had damaged certain brain cells, which affected my concept of shape and sense of direction as well as my sight. At that time neither I nor the teachers realised this, and all similarly affected children were told off for being slow and not managing to keep up with others.

We didn't work very fast at my boarding school and so I had no trouble in keeping up academically, but learning braille took quite a long time. There are a lot of contractions or abbreviations to cut down the bulkiness of braille, and we had to be introduced to them gradually over a period of four years.

I had always loved hearing stories and my greatest desire was to read an interesting book myself. At that time most of the braille readers were simple and not very imaginative. Because some of the girls took a long time to learn the abbreviations, they slowed the whole class down and I found this frustrating. Education for the blind has improved a great deal now and better teaching methods are used, but I owe a great deal to Lickey Grange School, who gave us all a good knowledge of basic subjects.

By the time I was nine or ten I had mastered braille enough to be able to pick up and read any book I fancied and I read lots of fairy stories which a sighted child would have discovered years previously. I became one of the best braille readers in my class and when I was ten I was chosen to read to the Queen Mother when she visited the school. It was a passage from *Peter Pan in Kensington Gardens* which apparently was one of her favourite pieces and I felt very important.

Because I wanted my parents to think I had been especially favoured by the royal visitor, I told them that the Queen Mother had paid more attention to me than she really had, and had come up to me especially to say, "Goodbye school and goodbye Marilyn". I think they believed me!

Friendships between the girls were important at school but feelings could get hurt. A girl called Sue James and I got on well together but one day we had a heated argument and she accused me of just using her friendship. In a way this was true, because as she was partially sighted she found her way around school more easily than I did, so I often tagged along with her. It was much simpler than trying to find my own way.

Sue and I managed to get over our disagreement. We remained good friends and she was always ready to help me out. In maths, a subject Sue was good at, we paired together and had to finish the textbook at the same time - the teacher didn't realise that I wasn't doing much of the work!

Around this time, some of the other girls began to talk about programmes they had 'watched' on television at home. Not to be outdone I asked Mum and Dad if we could have a TV.

"We didn't get one because we thought you would feel left out love," they explained. I appreciated their consideration but when they heard that other blind girls 'watched' television we soon had one installed at home. Over the years both Mum and Dad became expert at describing what happened on the screen so that the programmes, especially the films, really came alive to me.

Musically, I wasn't progressing very well and this frustrated Mum and Dad because they knew I had a musical gift. From an early age, I could play a tune on my grandmother's piano. As far as I was concerned, this was the highlight of our monthly visit to Fladbury, the picturesque Worcestershire village where she lived. I delighted in being able to pick out tunes and play pop songs. We didn't have a piano at home until I was eight or nine but I often sang or hummed tunes I heard on the radio and I had a good sense of rhythm.

A next-door neighbour of ours loved music and once when I called in with Mum when I was quite young, I casually commented, "Aunty Mary your clock chimes on the note 'G'". She was surprised, but when we tested it on her piano, she found I was correct. At that time, I just assumed everyone knew musical notes and it was only later that I realised I had perfect pitch.

In spite of my lack of progress with piano lessons, it had always been my dream to become a really good musician. At school I daydreamed about joining the brass band and when I was about nine, during a weekend home visit, I announced that I was the youngest person who had ever been selected to join. Mum and Dad were obviously delighted, but I had to admit before I went back that I had made the whole thing up! They couldn't understand why, but I wanted it to happen so much that, being an imaginative person, I almost dreamed myself into believing it was true. Later I did join the brass band, but it wasn't as exciting as I thought it would be!

When I was nine I was given one of the most exciting presents I had ever had - a reel to reel tape recorder. The idea of being able to record my voice and play it back was very exciting but when I heard my pronounced Birmingham accent I was horrified. I couldn't use the machine on my own at first and it had to be left at home for weekends and holidays, but I soon mastered threading the tape and using the controls. Sometimes I would get the tape twisted and call Dad to put it straight for me - often while he was watching a good film on TV, so at times he found my new interest a little exasperating! Because I dropped microphones on the floor several times we had to replace them, but it was a marvellous piece of equipment which really fired my imagination. I spent hours recording programmes like *Top of the Pops* and then dubbing in my voice as the D.J. introducing the records. At other times I altered my voice and became both the interviewer and the pop star. Sometimes I pretended to be an actress and performed my own radio plays with sound effects. It was all great fun!

Just before my tenth birthday, Dad said to me, "Marilyn, you don't seem to be getting on as well with the piano as you should. Is there another instrument you would like to learn?"

Mum enjoyed listening to the clarinet, so when I replied, "The oboe," she tried to persuade me to change my mind.

"Just think, if you played the clarinet, Marilyn, you'd be like Acker Bilk!"

But I was determined: I definitely wanted an oboe. Once Mum and Dad knew that I was serious, they went out to buy one for me. Not being musical themselves they didn't realise how difficult an oboe was to play: they expected me to get a note out of it straightaway and of course I couldn't!

A well-known oboe teacher in our area, Brenda Rees, started to give me lessons. After the first one, she commented to my Dad: "You know Mr. Baker, Marilyn is very gifted. She is going to be good and you ought to get her a better instrument."

Being the type of parents they were they did just that and I really enjoyed my Saturday morning lessons. Mum or Dad would pick me up from school and I would eat marmalade sandwiches in the front seat of the car.

One day in the school holidays that year, I happened to hear a sermon on the radio which really amazed me. The speaker said that God was interested in the smallest details of our lives: if we dropped something on the floor, He knew about it and cared. To me this was wonderful news because I was always dropping things, so from then on I would go down on my knees and say a little prayer before I felt around for what I'd lost. When Mum noticed this she said, "You don't need to pray about everything, love. God's got a lot to do and that's too small a thing to pray about. He hasn't time to hear all these kinds of prayers."

I thought that Mum knew best so I stopped praying, but with a sense of disappointment. That Easter on television there was a film about the crucifixion of Jesus. He seemed such a kind person and I cried at the thought of Him dying. Mum responded, "It does seem sad, love. I don't know why such a good man should die like that." I couldn't understand it - and neither Mum nor Dad, it seemed, could explain to me what it meant.

# Three

# A Long Way From Home

It was now time to think about moving to another school and both my parents and the staff at Lickey Grange had high hopes that I would get into Chorleywood College for the Blind in Hertfordshire. It was the only grammar school for blind girls offering 'O' and 'A' levels and was therefore very prestigious.

Only selected pupils could sit the entrance exam and this made me feel under pressure. My Dad had often said to me, "If you're going to get anywhere, you've got to do better than the average sighted person". Both my parents felt, in their love and concern for me, that I needed good academic qualifications if I was to make anything of my life, and I felt I owed it to them to pass.

The great day came and I went to Chorleywood for the exam, but I found the paper very difficult. I completely lost my nerve and gave stupid answers to simple questions - when asked, "What's the feminine for bull?" I wrote down "Bulless"! This was the first real exam I had taken in my life and what a mess I made of it.

Mum and Dad were very disappointed when I didn't get in to the school but in a way I was relieved: it meant that I wouldn't have to leave all my friends. There would be another chance for me to sit the exam in twelve months time and during that year I was specially tutored with specimen exam papers.

Amidst all this extra studying I was getting ready for something else which I found far more exciting. I was doing very well on the oboe and after I had been learning for a year Brenda Rees said to me, "My father runs a youth orchestra in Blackpool and I should like you to go and play as their guest soloist".

This was a great privilege and I learnt a concerto by Pengolesi for the occasion. Mum came with me to the Winter Gardens in Blackpool for the Saturday evening concert. To Dad's disappointment, he couldn't come as he had to look after the garage. After my performance the applause was terrific and being only ten or eleven at the time, I lapped up the attention and praise heaped on me. I was interviewed by reporters. Asked how it felt being famous, I replied, "Wonderful"! Mum and Dad thought my career was set fair - I was almost a child prodigy.

While rehearsing for the concert I had got to know Mr. Rees, my music teacher's father, quite well. Brenda Rees had told my parents that he was a Christian Scientist but they didn't really understand what this meant. Mr. Rees started talking to me about his faith and introduced me to some people from his church.

I was attracted by these people: they had a special unity and seemed so close to one another, really caring about each other's needs. Although I didn't understand a great deal about their beliefs I knew they didn't smoke or drink and that they didn't use doctors, as they believed that God would heal them. It was the first time I had met people with such a strong faith. They had a real sense of being in touch with a power beyond themselves and this impressed me.

Feeling that I needed something to believe in, I decided I wanted to become a Christian Scientist. My parents did not oppose me, although they said it was not something they could do themselves, but they wanted me to wait, especially after Miss Rees explained to them what was involved. She warned me against joining so young and it was decided that I should not make any commitment immediately.

It wasn't easy because for at least six months I had a

strong yearning to know more about this group of people who really did believe in miracles of healing and whose faith joined them together in a special way. I envied their sense of fulfilment and longed to be part of them. Gradually however, my interest cooled. I became absorbed in other things and my search for God was later to take me in a rather different direction.

The time soon came round for me to retake the Chorleywood College entrance exam. I felt calmer than I had done the year before as I knew better what was expected of me. Fortunately all my hard work paid off, and this time I passed.

I had mixed feelings about going further away from my parents so when September 1962 came and I started my first term I was both excited and frightened. My first impression was of a huge complicated building and grounds. I felt panic coming on at times and wondered how on earth I was going to learn my way around. At first the teachers were understanding as they realised it would take a little while to get used to the layout, but because of my problem with direction, I was much slower than many of the others. We all had to undergo walking tests. This meant that older girls taught us new routes and we were tested by a teacher walking behind us. We began on simple routes inside the school grounds and then went on to more difficult walks - first to the local shop and then into the village.

There were two drives in the school and one dreadful day the Headmistress asked those of us in the first year to go down the front drive and back again. I had never mastered which was the front drive and which the back and consequently I went the wrong way - the others didn't !

The Head was very cross with me. "You've been here two months now Marilyn, and you don't know the difference between the front and back drive," she shouted.

This really knocked my confidence: I still thought my problems with direction were due to my stupidity rather than to damaged brain cells and I was ashamed of my failure. I made a special effort to learn my way around the school and several months later I repeated the test and was successful. Unbeknown to me, films had been taken on both occasions. On the first I looked worried and confused, whereas on the second I appeared confident. Because of this I was used as an example of what a blind person can achieve in a fairly short period of time.

It was very difficult for me to settle at Chorleywood. I was used to being at the top of the class, but now I really struggled to keep up. It was a shock to my system and left me feeling insecure and inferior. The school was much larger than Lickey Grange and I didn't feel like an individual any more - now I was just one child among many. I felt very insignificant and was desperate for people to take notice of me.

The girls at school came from many different backgrounds, but a high social standard was expected of us all once we arrived at the school. We were encouraged to speak correctly and to lose our regional accents.

My biggest disappointment was that I could not continue to have oboe lessons. The Headmistress felt that my first year at grammar school would require a lot of academic work, leaving little time for extra music. And since no-one else was learning the oboe, the school didn't have a teacher. I continued to have lessons with Brenda Rees in the school holidays and kept up my playing during term-time.

I missed my weekend trips home and although Mum and Dad came down once a month to see me, we could only spend a few hours on a Sunday together.

Mum would always bring a picnic and we would sit in the car on Chorleywood Common to eat it.

Being so far away from Mum and Dad I felt in need of attention from other quarters, so I decided to write myself nasty letters, threatening to 'rip up your homework', as if they had come from someone in the sixth form. Some of the teachers were very sympathetic and of course it caused a great buzz in the school. Everyone was interested in me but my rise to fame was short-lived: even though I had gone to a lot of trouble to disguise who had written the letters, my identity was soon discovered and the whole thing died a natural death.

There was a good side to boarding school as well and we enjoyed having midnight feasts and playing jokes on each other. Desperately wanting people to like me, I would pretend to believe the most absurd things. I became the form fool and everyone thought me gullible. I acted out the part well and this gained me friends and, in a peculiar way, popularity as well. It was important for me to feel in the centre of things, but I really needed one special friend. I often felt lonely and during the times we were encouraged to go for walks in the grounds or to do things in pairs I would be on my own, which increased my feelings of insecurity.

Another way I tried to gain popularity was by writing stories. I entitled them *The fate of ......* and they were sometimes about teachers or senior girls. Often the girls in my year would beg me to write a 'fate' story for them.

After my first year, I won a prize for progress because I had improved in all aspects of my work. In recognition of this the Head arranged for me to have oboe lessons again. My new teacher was called Miss Fisher. She was excellent, very strict, and made sure I practised regularly. I thought of her as being a slave driver because I was too lazy to like this! Miss Fisher recognised my gift and wanted to make sure that I made the most of my talent. Dad became very interested in my oboe playing and at the end of each term this was the most important report as far as he was concerned. Fortunately, it was nearly always a good one.

I was looking forward to going home for the Christmas holidays in 1963 and was particularly excited about seeing Nan Lou. The good relationship we had shared when I was younger had continued, but this time it was different because she was going to Bournemouth soon to live with my aunt and uncle. I realised how much I would miss her, so I wanted to spend as much of this holiday as I could with her.

I didn't realise that anything was wrong until Mum stood in the kitchen when we got home and said, "Love I've got something to tell you". She paused and said, with concern in her voice, "Your Nan is very poorly - she's had a stroke and she's in hospital, but she wants to see you". A cold shudder went through me as I stood speechless. It was the first time I had come into contact with serious illness and I felt lost, unsure how to cope.

When I went to visit Nan she couldn't speak but she could hear, so I told her to squeeze my hand once if she wanted to reply 'yes' and twice for 'no', and that was how we communicated. I think it made us both feel closer. It was difficult to hold back the tears, but Mum kept telling me not to cry in front of Nan as it would upset her, and for a thirteen year old this was not easy. I felt as if my heart was going to break with sadness. Her rattling breathing frightened me, and being aware of Nan lying there so helpless made me realise how much I hated frailty, old age and suffering. It was obvious that she was slipping away from me and it was hard that I could do nothing about it. I realised that soon she would be gone and I wouldn't be able to share my secrets with her anymore. My thoughts went back to lying in bed with her as a little girl and saying, "Nan, if you find out what happens when we die, will you come back and tell me?" And she had said, "Of course I will love, if I can". Because I knew she loved me, I had quite expected that she would.

Just after Christmas she died. As we made New Year's resolutions at the beginning of 1964 I felt that the coming year would be the worst I would ever have to face. The funeral service was in a little chapel at Wittern cemetery. It was cold and bleak. The vicar tried to comfort us and quoted words from the Bible which seemed irrelevant and old-fashioned to me. Mum was obviously sad too at the loss of her mother but she knew how good a relationship Nan and I had had and she said, "I'll try and make up for it love. I know how much you loved your Nan."

It was around this time that people at school were discussing whether to be confirmed. I thought this might be a good idea: perhaps there was a God who could be of some help to me. So I started going along to the school confirmation classes, but I felt we had to believe a lot of 'religious' things which didn't have much bearing on everyday life, and it was so dreary.

Sundays were boring at school and so was compulsory church attendance, but deep inside I felt that God, although I didn't know how, ought to be important. Instinctively I believed that He was somewhere looking after us in some way. When I was eventually confirmed, one of the hymns we sang was *Oh Jesus, I have Promised to Serve You to the End*, and although I didn't fully understand what that meant, I agreed with the sentiment and earnestly wanted God to be involved somehow in my life.

In the village of Forge near Machynlleth our family had a beautiful cedarwood chalet built. It was within easy driving distance of the coast, quite close to where we used to have our caravan, and was the perfect place to spend holidays. I adored it and loved the smell of cedarwood. I have very happy memories of the many hours Mum and I spent on the beaches in Wales. We would often sit down by the harbour in Aberystwyth eating fish and chips, or go climbing on the sand dunes. It was like being in a different world from school and it made me forget the sad and difficult things for a time.

Ever since arriving at Chorleywood, I had developed severe stomach pains. Sometimes they were really crippling, and I went for a number of tests at the hospital but no reason could be found for them. They often came and went, which meant that I had to lie down during the day. Occasionally I used them as an excuse for not doing something and one day I lost a piece of music which I should have learnt for my oboe lesson, so I said I had a bad pain and made myself sick in the cloakroom. I was put to bed as usual and, of course, missed my lesson. I expected to get up later but instead, the school called the doctor in. He thought I might have appendicitis and sent me to a specialist. I was prodded about and, of course, felt extremely nervous, because on this occasion the pains weren't genuine. The specialist said he couldn't find much wrong, but wanted a second opinion. I was prodded about again and kept insisting that the pains were less and I felt much better, but nobody took any notice. The doctors decided that since I had been troubled with these pains for quite a while, and my 'O' levels would be coming up shortly, the best thing would be to remove my appendix, which was normal procedure in those days.

I went into hospital and was terrified in case I would

spill the beans while under the anaesthetic. Altogether, I missed about five weeks of school and enjoyed convalescing at home with Mum and Dad, but I did miss Nan Lou at that time.

During my stay in hospital, Mum and Dad thought it time I had a better class of oboe and they bought me a professional one, made by T.W. Howorth of London - it was one of the best and even now I would have difficulty replacing it. I wanted to try it out but couldn't while I was in hospital because the operation wound hurt. I enjoyed playing it a great deal once I got home and this helped pass the time.

It turned out that my appendix wasn't the reason for the stomach pains after all, because in spite of the operation, they did continue. In the end the doctor said it was due to nerves and called it 'migraine of the stomach'.

# Four

# Searching

Just after I returned to school I became good friends with Susan Moore, a New Zealander who was living in Britain for a year. We got up to all kinds of pranks and it was the closest friendship I had made at this school. Having been at boarding school from the age of five meant that I didn't have many friends at home, so holidays were sometimes quite lonely. It was a great thrill when Sue came to stay with me or I could go to her for part of the holidays.

Sue felt that because she wasn't English she wasn't as accepted as some of the other girls, so we devised a heroic plan where I would fall into the swimming pool (accidentally on purpose) and Sue would rescue me. She would then be a heroine! The trouble was it was almost winter and I suddenly realised it was going to be very chilly. I had heard that long distance swimmers smeared grease all over their bodies to keep out the cold so I covered myself with Nivea cream. When it actually came to jumping in the pool I lost my nerve, because I was afraid Sue wouldn't find me, and I was not a strong swimmer. She wasn't very amused when I wouldn't fulfil my part of the plan, but it didn't affect our friendship!

I had always been interested in the supernatural and had a curiosity about spiritualism, so I persuaded Sue to join me in an experiment. We crept up to the surgery and got two glasses which we took to the cellar. We wanted to see if we could get them to move when we put our hands on them, but when they did it really frightened us. At that time I just thought it was good fun and didn't realise the dangers of dabbling in such things.

At that time a girl in our form, Judith, had started a Christian club. She called it the YPF which, Sue insisted, meant Young Poultry Farmers instead of Young People's Fellowship! Sue and I went along, more out of curiosity than anything else. Judith's parents were missionaries in Zambia and one day she heard that her brother had been killed. It was a terrible shock to her and affected her badly. She wanted to get away from anything which reminded her of her home, family and their Christian commitment. On Sundays Judith had been going to visit a couple connected with her parents' church. Feeling as she did she asked me if I would like to visit Mr and Mrs Bannard-Smith sometimes instead. I thought this a very good idea, as it would be a change to get away from school over the weekend.

I could tell from the outset that there was something different about the Bannard-Smiths and it wasn't just that they were religious. They treated Sunday as a special day and when they said grace, it wasn't just the old 'rattled-off' school prayer - they really talked to God as if He was there in the room. One evening they invited me to their church. It was very different from anything I had ever been to before - not the traditional hymn singing, with constant standing up and sitting down. The hymns were lively, not slow and dreary as I had come to expect, and people prayed as if they were talking to a person - someone they knew.

I was invited to the young people's meeting after church, so I went along. Again the singing was lively - people were clapping their hands and really enjoying themselves, and they chatted naturally about Jesus Christ as if He was right there with them. They spoke of their everyday problems and how they could talk to Jesus about them. I was amazed at their certainty. To me Jesus had always been someone in a stained glass window, a historical character with no reality for today. These people seemed sure that He was more than just an ordinary man.

But could they prove this? At school, when we'd heard accounts of His miracles I had always thought they were like fairy stories and had never taken them too seriously. "Why did Jesus die?" I wondered, "and how could He have come back from the dead as the Bible says?" I really wanted to find out whether these things were true, but I had no idea where to look for the answers.

During this time an amazing thing happened - a parcel arrived at school for me. When I opened it, it was a braille magazine from the United States and the title was *The Overwhelming Proof Of The Divinity Of Jesus*. I hadn't a clue who could possibly have asked for something in braille for me, but I started reading. The magazine went through Old Testament passages promising that God's Son would come into our world as the God-Man and it also showed the Scriptures on His second coming. I read and studied the Bible verses in the magazine - the only way I could have done so because a braille Bible takes up about six feet of shelf space. If I had had to look up other reference books as well, it would have taken me a very long time! By reading these passages grouped together I began to realise that what Jesus had said about Himself was true. I knew an inward feeling of certainty and rightness, stronger than anything I had ever experienced.

I found a book in the school chapel called *The Transforming Friendship* by Leslie Weatherhead. It was the title that drew me and the book made a great impression on me. It portrayed Jesus as a real person with real feelings and a deep understanding of people and of life. Could it really be possible for me to know Jesus as the kind of friend this book talked about? I was beginning to long to know whether this could happen.

Around this time Judith, who was still feeling the sadness of her brother's death, asked me if I would take over from her as leader of the YPF at school. I didn't want to let a good club come to an end, so even though I had no experience of leadership I accepted the challenge. To lead the discussions, I found that I had to study the Bible more than I had done before.

Sue Moore had returned to New Zealand by this time and her going had left a gap in my life - and hers! We wrote long letters in braille telling each other all that we were doing and for some time we missed each other a great deal. I would have loved to be able to share my thoughts and new discoveries with her, but they were difficult to put down on paper.

I started going along regularly to the Bannard-Smiths' church on a Sunday evening and I would sometimes go on a Sunday morning as well.This service was very different. It was called 'the breaking of bread', a form of holy communion where the bread was passed round from one person to another. Before that took place, people would thank God quite simply and sincerely for the forgiveness they had experienced. One day someone prayed, "Thank You Lord because I know that when I die I am going to be with You in heaven".

I was indignant at this remark. Getting into the car with Doris Bannard-Smith I said, "I think that man's a real bighead, saying that he knows he's going to heaven. Nobody can know that - you can only hope that if you're good enough you'll make it somehow."

Her reply came as a total surprise to me. "No Marilyn, it's not like that," she said. "We can never be good enough for God. We might think we're alright because we're better than other people, but when we compare ourselves with God, Who is absolutely perfect, we can never make it. Being right with God has got nothing to do with how hard we try, it's actually a gift that God gives." This was all new to me and I sat thinking about it all through lunch.

That afternoon Doris opened her Bible and read me a verse in John's Gospel: "For God so loved the world that he gave his one and only Son, that whoever believes in him shall not perish but have everlasting life." Very simply, Doris went through this verse phrase by phrase, explaining to me what it meant.

"'For God so loved the world,'" Doris said. "That means not only that He loves the world He has made, but that He cares about everybody in it."

I nodded in agreement and then she said, "So that includes you Marilyn. He loves you very much." Doris paused for a moment, letting the words sink in.

This was mind-blowing! I had always thought of God as a remote and distant being, but if this was true it meant that He cared about me. I wasn't just one of the crowd, to Him I was someone special.

"Without God we lose our way and have no purpose in life," Doris went on. "But Jesus came into our world to bring us into a close relationship with God."

"How can He do that?" I asked.

"We can never get close to God by our own efforts," Doris told me. "We are separated from Him by all the wrong things we've done. But when Jesus died on the cross He took the punishment we deserved for every single one of those wrong things, so we need never be cut off from God again. If we accept what Jesus has done we can know God personally and have life for ever - even after we die."

"Does that include me?" I asked. "Can I be sure of everlasting life?"

"Yes Marilyn you can," Doris replied.

Billy Graham came to England at this time and I thought that he was preaching at the local Baptist Church in Rickmansworth. I went along with some other girls from school and was a little disappointed to find that it wasn't Billy Graham himself, but another member of his team. Many of the questions I had been thinking about that week, however - whether I could really know God; whether He was real; whether He would do what He promised - were answered by that evangelist.

"Faith is rather like sitting on a chair," he said. "It's no good just looking at it, you have to sit down on it believing it's going to hold you up. In the same way, once you begin trusting God you will start finding His promises true in your experience."

He said that every wrong thing we had done could be forgiven and forgotten by God and it was staggering to appreciate what that meant. "God doesn't just want us to cope as best we can," the evangelist went on. "He has a plan for each of us and He wants to help and guide us through life as our loving Father."

I felt like bursting with the excitement of this. It was wonderful and new and I was thrilled at all that I was hearing.

At the end of the meeting the speaker concluded, "Now if anyone wants to know a Father-son or Father-daughter relationship with God, just raise your hand and I will pray with you at the end of the meeting". I did put up my hand, but as we were whisked back to school as soon as the service was over, nobody was able to pray with me.

That night, I remembered how the evangelist had quoted a verse from the Bible: "If you confess your sins I will make you clean from every wrong". He had said that if we asked the Holy Spirit, Who is God's energy, power and personality, to come into our lives, He would do so. He had also quoted Revelation chapter 3 verse 20: "Behold I stand at the door and knock. If anyone opens the door, I will come in."

I really wanted this personal relationship with God that the evangelist was talking about, so I knelt down by my bed in the school dormitory and talked to God in a way I had never done before:

"Lord I know my life hasn't been all that it should be. Please forgive me for my selfish thoughts, my wrong motives, my unhelpfulness, my temper and all that kind of thing. Thank You Lord that You will forgive me and that You have got a plan for my life."

I had an indescribable feeling of peace and a quiet joy. I knew that God had heard me and had a real sense of His presence in the room. Later though, a little doubt crept into my mind: "If I go to bed and wake up tomorrow, will it all be over? Will it just be like a dream?"

But when I did wake I realised that God was my Father and companion, and Jesus was really with me. I remembered his words, "I will never leave you nor forsake you". It was wonderful: God was no longer on the outside of my life, I felt His love deep inside me.

I had given myself wholly to Him and He was totally committed to me. This relationship has meant so much to me throughout my life. Although I've let Him down many times since, I know that He's never let go of my hand.

It didn't really occur to me that I was a particularly bad person. In fact I thought that I was quite good, and when I confessed my sin that night and asked God to forgive me, I didn't think there was a lot that I needed to be forgiven for. Over a period of time, though, God gently and definitely pointed out some wrong attitudes. Telling lies had never bothered me, especially when it was to my advantage or stopped me getting into trouble, so I did it without thinking.

One of the strict rules at school was that we weren't allowed radios in our dormitories, but no prizes for guessing who had one upstairs! We heard via the grapevine that the care assistants were going to do a spot check one morning so I dashed to the dorm hoping to get my radio downstairs without it being detected. To my consternation I found one of the assistants standing with my radio in her hand. She demanded crisply what I was doing by having it upstairs. "Well actually it hasn't any batteries in it," I replied. She didn't believe me and switched it on. It *did* have batteries, but I knew she wouldn't get any sound out of it because I had switched on to a special wave band that would only work with the aerial attached.

She said, "Oh well in that case, I'll give it to the head matron and she'll probably give it you back later". I went downstairs congratulating myself and thinking how clever I had been. But something happened inside my heart. It was as if the sense of quiet and peace began to depart from me and I said instinctively, "Lord, where are You? I can't seem to sense You so close." Straight back came the answer: "Marilyn, you've disappointed Me." For the first time in my life I felt really convicted about telling a lie and sad that I'd disappointed the One I was growing to love - the One Who loved me so much. I went straight back upstairs and owned up to the fact that there *were* batteries in the radio set and I'd been using it to listen to Billy Graham. The care staff were so startled at my honesty that they they gave me the radio straight back. My change of heart astonished them!

The Lord also challenged me about jealousy. There was a girl in my class who was very musical and she was often asked to play the piano, for instance in school assemblies. I thought I was better than she was, and I didn't see why she should be chosen so often!

I used some daily Bible reading notes in braille, by the Bible Reading Fellowship, which gave a few verses to read and then added a comment. One day the topic was jealousy and I felt God was showing me that I had to stop envying this particular girl. I prayed that God would forgive me, and that He would change my attitude towards Julie. I'd often tried to 'turn over a new leaf' in the past and it hadn't worked. Even though I had prayed, I can't have expected too dramatic a change, because the next morning I had forgotten about it! I went outside for what we called 'Garden Ex', short for garden exercise, when we just strolled around the grounds. We usually went with our friends, but this particular morning I was on my own and I bumped into Julie. She was also alone, and very upset because she had had a letter from her brother with some sad news. We chatted about this and when I came in from the walk I thought, "I hope I can get to know Julie better. She really is a lovely person." It was only when I went into assembly later that my mind was jogged and I remembered my prayer of the day before. I was amazed that my attitude had changed so dramatically. God had really answered.

# Five

# Sixth Form Freedom

When I was fifteen the school asked me what kind of career I was thinking of taking up. I replied that, as my oboe playing had developed considerably, I would like to become a professional oboist. As I was the first blind pupil who had ever had such an ambition, they felt that a second opinion was needed. My teacher, Miss Fisher, knew the famous oboist Terence McDonna, and was a great admirer of his work. He was mainly a chamber music player, but he also played with the B.B.C. Symphony Orchestra. She wrote and asked him if he would give his opinion on my playing, and he graciously agreed to come to the school.

My friend and music teacher Jean Coates accompanied me on the piano. Jean and I had built up a close musical rapport and had spent many happy hours playing together. She brought the music alive for me, and I felt inspired when playing with her. It was a duo that I found could never be repeated, and in it both of us found a wonderful fulfilment. We thoroughly enjoyed performing for Terence McDonna, but even so I was quite nervous. His comments were encouraging however, and he said that I should definitely continue with the oboe.

Round about the time I took my 'O' levels Miss Fisher left the school to join the Hallé Orchestra, and it was only after she had gone that I realised how much I had taken her for granted. I hadn't done as much work as I could or should have done. She had been an excellent teacher, and I tried hard to remember what she had told me.

I sat for seven 'O' levels and passed them all, even General Science, which was my worst subject. I felt pleased with my results, and knew Mum and Dad were pleased as well.

That summer during the holidays, I became more interested in shopping. Mum used to take me into town on the bus and we would go bargain hunting in the sales. Colour doesn't mean anything to me. Many blind people have some concept of light and dark and if they have seen before going blind they can understand colours, but there is no light and dark in my world. I am not 'living in the dark' as some people suggest, because I have not seen light. It is all the same - normal.

Mum would tell me which colours were fashionable and which ones suited me. I was dependent on what she thought looked right on me and I was always anxious not to look old-fashioned. If I had tried to choose for myself I would have got into difficulties, choosing either the wrong style or the wrong colour combinations. So I had to accept that I would wear what Mum thought best and was pleased when sighted people complimented me on my appearance.

The other exciting thing which happened during those holidays was that I perfected my recording techniques on a stereo multi-track tape recorder Mum and Dad bought me. Dad showed me how to work it and I soon recorded one instrument on top of another, putting together some lovely effects. The concept fascinated me and I harmonised with myself and recorded myself singing and playing the piano. Helen Shapiro, who had a low voice like mine, was making hit records at the time. I tried to perform like her and actually won a talent competition doing it.

It wasn't easy to find a replacement for Miss Fisher and when I returned to school after the holidays I was without an oboe teacher for a while. The school wrote to Terence McDonna asking whether any of his students would be able to come and teach me, or if he knew of anyone else suitable. He replied to say that he would come himself - I could hardly believe it! He was a professor at the Royal College of Music and that was the college I was hoping to get into. It seemed too good to be true. Sometimes Jean Coates and I went to his home for lessons and at other times he came to the school. Usually I had lessons once a month and I felt it a tremendous privilege to be taught by such a genius. After I had been taught by him for a while I heard that he didn't like teaching women, but he seemed very willing to teach me and his lessons were a real inspiration. Because they were not regular, Jean Coates helped a great deal by putting many of the pieces into braille for me. Braille music is nothing like printed music and does not have five lines and spaces. There are different combinations of dots for each note up the scale and a special sign tells which octave that note is in. The octaves are numbered from the bottom and middle C is the fourth octave. The value of the note - crotchets, quavers and so on - is indicated by a different set of dots. Each note has to be read separately and then memorised. The whole system is very complicated and laborious to learn and I will always be grateful to Jean for her invaluable help.

Instead of being in dormitories in the sixth form, we were able to move into a new building called Cedar House Flatlets which Princess Margaret came to open. I was put in charge of a little choir who would sing Mozart's Ave Verum just as she came past the music room for the ceremony. Jean Coates had put the piano accompaniment onto a tape and I was to switch this on when we were about to sing. Unfortunately I rubbed part of it off the tape! It was just before the Royal visitor arrived so I tried to get the group of girls to sing from the middle of the Ave Verum onwards. It was really difficult to achieve but it worked!

In Cedar House we had little flatlets with either double or single rooms and a kitchen. This meant that we had a lot of independence and became better equipped for adult life.

One of my craziest ideas was to run a radio station which I called *Radio Cedar House*. I had always liked the idea of radio stations and playing with tape recorders. When I was twelve or thirteen I had tried to make my own local radio station at home and discovered that for some strange reason, if I connected my tape recorder to my radio in a certain way, what I had taped would come through the radio. It could be heard on the radio downstairs and also next door, though the reception there was poor. Mum had been worried we would get into trouble with the Post Office! I had made up signature tunes for my own B.B.C. Radio Hansworth and also advertisements for my Dad's garage.

These activities had fired my imagination and now at Cedar House I put the loudspeaker from my big tape recorder outside my room so that my friends could call out messages through a microphone. The sound echoed round the whole of the building, and needless to say I got told off about the terrible noise!

I suppose I was a bit of a ringleader at school. I had three good friends, the two Margarets and Penny. Margaret Ellison played the violin and was keen on classical music, which she encouraged me to listen to on the radio. Her enthusiasm rubbed off on me and I now love listening to the violin, especially concertos.

Margaret Wilson was a studious girl and extremely good at science. She was a born teacher who made a subject come alive and it was she who helped me with my 'O' level science. Penny Cooze, who later came to live with me in Watford, was the quietest of us all. She was a sensitive girl and because of her family circumstances, couldn't always go home for holidays. This meant that her years at school weren't very easy for her.

I had some problems myself when I decided to take Scripture as well as Music 'A' level. The Scripture course, I found, was liberal in its teaching and we had to read books which were very critical of the Bible. The set texts were Romans and Jeremiah so I discovered a lot about the Lord's love for me during those 'A' level lessons, but I also began to find that my faith was being undermined as I read disparaging essays on the make-up of the Bible. I realised that I wasn't at the stage where I could cope with that kind of material, so after discussing it with Jean Coates, I decided to give up the 'A' level Scripture course. This seemed a drastic step, but I felt it was more important to maintain my newfound faith than get an 'A' level. Had I been a Christian longer, I would have been able to think through the issues more constructively. Interestingly enough, on the day the 'A' level took place, I was ill with a bad stomach bug and would have been unable to take the exam.

All through the years at school I had been taking piano and oboe exams. A blind person can't read and play music at the same time. We have to go through the slow process of reading and committing to memory each bar written in braille, first learning the left and right hand separately and then together.

In music exams, instead of the 'sight reading test' a special 'memory test' is devised for blind students. A short simple piece of music is played and the blind person plays back a single line which he or she has had to remember.

Learning braille music is terribly complicated and a lot of people don't try but simply play by ear. Accurate phrasing and expression however, can only be achieved when the music has been read and learned. Sighted people can usually pass a sight reading exam even if they are not very musical but blind people cannot - they have to have a good musical 'ear'. Many people assume that all blind people are musical automatically but this is certainly not the case. A good memory is essential and braille music is no good if you haven't got that.

In the sixth form I achieved the grade eight oboe exam with a high distinction mark, which qualified me to enter for the special scholarship offered by the Associated Board of the Royal Schools of Music. Jean Coates told me the she felt there was very little chance of me getting anywhere near the semi-final because of the hundreds of people entering. We were given set pieces and I had to play an extremely difficult work for the oboe by a composer called York Bowen. This was a struggle and taxed me to my limit, but it was also very satisfying to get to grips with it.

Studying for two 'A' levels would have been extremely difficult because I had to spend such a long time practising both piano and oboe, learning harmony and theory and working towards the exam. Jean was amazed when I reached the semi-final for the Associated Boards scholarship and besides being a real thrill for me, it gave my confidence a boost. I then took the entrance exam for the Royal College of Music and was given an interview. I was delighted, and so were my parents, when I was accepted and given a grant.

Though life for me was exciting, for my friend Penny this was a difficult time. I discovered that she had in fact taken an overdose. We had been led to believe that she had been ill with a stomach bug, but later on she confided in me that she had been feeling so desperate that she had tried to end it all. I suddenly became aware that I had been living in cloud cuckoo land. I had never realised that anyone could be as unhappy as that and it awakened me to my responsibilities as a Christian. I saw how important it was for Penny to find the love of God for herself. She was a Catholic but it was the beauty of the ceremony and the ritual which she was hanging onto rather than any personal relationship with God. Penny started to come along with me to St. Andrews church and I began to pray earnestly that God would help me in whatever way I could to show her what it really meant to become a Christian.

Chorleywood College was an excellent school, but there is no doubt that a boarding school for the blind is a sheltered environment. Apart from outings with the school and activities in the holidays, we didn't venture much into the outside world.

The school held a reunion every three years, which

coincided with the year I left. I was asked to help out when the old girls came back for the weekend and had a super time hearing about the things that some of them had been doing. One had even got a job as a teacher in a comprehensive school. Listening to their talk made me wonder how I would cope with life outside school, but I was determined to make a go of it.

Once I became a Christian I went with a neighbour to a Pentecostal Church in Graham Street, Birmingham during the school holidays, but found it difficult to get to know others of my own age there. Mum and Dad seemed to accept my being a Christian but appeared to think it was just a phase of growing up, so they didn't discourage my new 'interest'!

The first real contact I had with sighted teenagers was when I went on an Inter-Schools Christian Fellowship camp run by Scripture Union for blind, partially-sighted and sighted girls. I learnt such a lot at that camp. Many of the people involved in it as staff members are now good friends of mine. Margaret Atkin was the leader and on one memorable occasion she caught me in the kitchen finishing off a very large portion of lemon meringue pie. I shouldn't think she had ever seen anyone with a mouth as full as mine!

Muriel Phillingham was the cook at the camp and she was also a home economics teacher. Much to my surprise she said to me one day, "Marilyn, I know that I can teach you how to cook: I've got every confidence in you".

At school my cookery skills were virtually nil. In fact I used to rush into the common room after the lesson and tell my friends the dreadful things that had happened in cookery that week. It was the highlight of our Fridays! Once I was supposed to be putting cabbage into a saucepan of boiling water and I put it in my friend's custard instead, and on two occasions I missed out the cheese in macaroni cheese! I had never found practical things easy and I really did feel a failure at cookery, but Muriel changed all that. She got me down in the kitchen and taught me how to make pies and cakes, as well as doing all sorts of things like stirring gallons of soup! Much to my surprise I began to enjoy cooking.

But what impressed me most about the camp was a girl about my own age called June Ramsden. Her whole life radiated love and I could tell that she loved God in a way I didn't. We became close friends and it didn't matter that she was sighted and I was blind. At first I thought she was only being kind to me, but later I realised it was more than that. She really enjoyed my company and I felt no sense of inequality with her. I came away from the camp feeling challenged to know more about God in the way June did. I had a new resolve to get to know Jesus better.

# Six

# The Big World

My faith was really tested once I knew I was going to the Royal College of Music in London. I had to find somewhere to live and a hostel just opposite the College seemed the sensible place to choose. I assumed that that was what my Heavenly Father had planned for me.

Jean Coates, my old music teacher, came with me to the hostel for an interview with the wardens, but they decided that I wouldn't be able to manage the numerous stairs, so I was refused a place. It was only then that I had to face the fact that people in the outside world were fearful of the responsibility of having a blind person in their care, and it hit me hard. I was deeply disappointed and almost felt God had let me down. "How could He want me to do a difficult walk in the busy streets of London?" I thought. I had never done a lot of walking on my own and the idea of coping with London traffic was daunting. After much searching we did find a place which was willing to have me but it was in Harrington Gardens, half an hour's walk from the college.

During the summer holidays of 1969 I stayed with Jean Coates for a week and we travelled to London each day so that I could practise the walk. I used a short white stick at the time and had to tap along the walls in order to find my way. (Nowadays the method is to use a long cane. We walk down the centre of the pavement and as our right foot goes forward our left hand goes round in an arch - then as our left foot goes forward our stick comes round to the right. This means that the stick comes into contact with any obstacle which needs to be avoided). During my week with Jean I gradually gained confidence practising the route, but I was concerned as to how I would manage without her walking beside me.

Mum and Dad were delighted when I was accepted for the Royal College of Music but were obviously concerned about my living in London. They were very appreciative of Jean's help in preparing me for city life. Their lives changed too that year as they moved into a Gothic style house. Dad converted the storeroom at the back into a comfortable bedroom for me, with its own gas fire and washbasin. I called it 'My Den' and it's still my favourite room - a very relaxing place to be.

That summer, it seemed incredible that I wouldn't be going back to Chorleywood College. Many of the people with whom I had spent so much time would no longer be part of my life and I had no idea what lay ahead.

September soon came, and Mum and Dad drove me to London to start my musical studies. We found Harrington Gardens after a while and discovered that I was to share a room with several foreign students. Not having had much to do with sighted people or those from other cultures before, I found it nerve-racking. Fortunately I was helped to settle in by the housekeeper Miss Banks, who was very good to me right from the beginning.

Mum told me afterwards that she was heartbroken at leaving me alone in the hostel. Both she and Dad were worried about how I would cope, but they knew that I needed to be independent, so neither of them communicated their concern to me. I didn't want them to know how frightened I was either, but when we said goodbye and they drove off down the road I felt very alone, left in a strange place with strange people.

There was a common room downstairs and other girls in the hostel asked me to go down and join them, but I wouldn't because I thought people were watching me. When I walked round, I sensed a kind of silence as the path was cleared for me, and this made me feel embarrassed and awkward. I was now in the world of sighted people. I was the odd one out and that was something I'd never had to deal with before.

Under the leadership of a new headmistress, Miss Marks, Chorleywood College started giving girls more contact with sighted people, so later students weren't quite as apprehensive of the outside world as I and many other girls of my age had been.

Eventually I settled down to life in the hostel but looking back now it seems strange to think that I regarded other young people as a threat! I am a naturally sociable person, so I didn't stay upstairs in the dormitory for long. I ventured into the common room and got to know some of my fellow lodgers.

On the first day of term I walked to the college with another girl. I arranged to meet her for the return trip to the hostel at half past four, because although I had done the route many times with Jean, the thought of walking it on my own still filled me with apprehension.

We were taken on a guided tour of the college and it seemed so big that I wondered how I would manage to find my way round. At the end of the day my mind was spinning and I made my way down to the canteen to meet my companion for the return home. I was feeling tired and overawed. One of the canteen staff brought me a cup of tea and I waited at the table. Twenty five to five... twenty to five ... ten to five ... five o'clock and there was no sign of this girl. The loneliness of my situation swept over me and I was almost paralysed with fear. I didn't know what to do. There was chattering and laughter going on all around me but I wasn't part of it - I was alone. This was the time to put my Christian faith to the test, I decided. I had not had to rely on God much before but now I needed Him and I prayed desperately - although I wasn't too sure if my prayer would be answered:

"Lord Jesus, if You are real then I ask You to help me

right now. Do something for me, please."

Just then somebody came and sat down opposite me. He asked me if I was one of the new students and introduced himself as Martin, the president of the Christian Union. I was overjoyed to meet him and told him about my predicament. God was certainly with me and had provided an answer to my prayer almost before I had asked Him! Martin decided the best thing was for him to follow me rather than walk with me, so that he could watch me do the route on my own. I managed this successfully and so regained my confidence.

I had known there was a Christian Union at the College because the Bannard-Smiths, who had nurtured me in my Christian faith, had told me they would write and tell the president I was coming. So it was really good to meet Martin on my first day.

As it turned out, my three years at the college were some of the happiest in my life. I found that I related to people much more easily than I had thought possible and I learnt a great deal about the reality of being a Christian. Right from the beginning different members of the Christian Union introduced themselves and invited me to go to their prayer meeting. My concept of prayer changed - any prayer meetings I had attended had only lasted for ten minutes or so but here at the college they lasted for an hour. At first I thought these people were a bit fanatical and I had reservations about going along, but when I did, I found that their relationship with God was very real. Prayer wasn't a formal set-up - we talked to a living God. These meetings revitalised my idea of prayer and I eventually became prayer secretary of the Christian Union.

At weekends I often went to stay in Little Chalfont with Jean Coates and her friend Beryl Rodd, who had invited me to go and see them if ever I felt lonely. It wasn't too difficult a train journey for me. We used to go along to

St. Andrews Church Chorleywood on Sunday mornings, and I used to look forward to these occasions. In the winter evenings I loved to snuggle into one of Jean and Beryl's comfortable armchairs and often dropped off to sleep after a tiring week at college.

One day we held a hen party for one of Beryl's colleagues who was getting married. I sat down in my favourite armchair after a scrumptious meal and fell asleep. Jean shook me awake about two hours later and informed me that the party was over and that I had issued loud snores, much to everyone's amusement!

# Seven

# Freedom to Travel

Living not far from Gloucester Road tube station was very handy for me because I was able to go and meet friends in different parts of London. If I had lived near college in the original hostel I had thought suitable, I would not have had the freedom or confidence to do this. I found it thrilling to travel by tube and was able to enjoy many outings with my friends.

Even though my walks to and from college became easier, I didn't find them relaxing and sometimes it was quite an effort to maintain my concentration. On several occasions the white stick I used broke because someone - usually a young man - rushed out of his house and tripped over it. When this happened I was stranded so I had to get these young men to take me back to the hostel or to the college. It got to be quite a joke with my friends, who said that it was a good way of picking up a young man in London!

There were no other blind students at the Royal College at this time, so no special facilities were provided for me. I recorded lectures on cassette and had to translate them into braille in the evenings. I couldn't do the degree course because there were no braille textbooks available. Nowadays students can ask for a lot more books to be put into braille for them and many are available on tape. It's much more difficult for blind people to read through material quickly because a page of braille can't be scanned like a printed page in order to get a grasp of the basic points.

I kept in touch with many old friends, including Penny Cooze. She was living in a hostel in the London area and still suffering from depression. At times she had to be admitted to a psychiatric hospital following a suicide attempt. When she was well she would come to see me in college. Sometimes one of the girls from the CU would escort us to the Wimpey. We usually got in a mess with the banana longboats but we enjoyed ourselves. When we were out walking we always used our sticks, but one day we were both knocked down when we were actually being guided across a road. Fortunately neither of us was badly hurt.

Penny came to the CU meetings at college and got to know a number of students, who started praying for her. At times she was too ill to come and visit me so I went to her, but CU members often remembered her in prayer.

Over the Christmas of my first year, romance began to bud. I had always been shy of boys and perhaps subconsciously felt that I would not be attractive to someone sighted. The college held a Christmas ball and a young man in the Christian Union called David, who had been particularly kind all term, invited me, much to my delight, to go with him. Others in the CU encouraged our relationship and we eventually started going out together.

David had a quiet, caring personality and had been a real friend from the beginning. He would often come to the canteen with me and help me get some lunch and find a seat, which I always found difficult. He lived in the boys' hostel of the college and was a clarinetist. Friends told me that he was handsome and I was very pleased, although looks don't matter to me as much as they do to people who can see. I think they can often be misled by outward appearances.

I felt great when David came to collect me at the hostel in the evenings, especially when I heard the call, "Marilyn, your boyfriend's here". He took an interest in my appearance and commented on the type of clothes he thought suited me, which made me take a new interest myself in how I looked. David and I became close friends and I shared with him all my problems, knowing that he understood. It was a new experience for me and a marvellous time in my life.

In the Christian Union people were beginning to talk about an experience called the Baptism of the Holy Spirit and about speaking in tongues. This is mentioned in the New Testament, where believers speak in a new language after the Holy Spirit has come upon them. Although I had heard about this kind of thing, I had dismissed it. I had gone to a Brethren-type church where it was felt that such experiences and practices represented an emotionalism which should be avoided. But now this was happening in the Christian Union and one day, to my astonishment, David told me that he had been baptised with the Holy Spirit.

I reacted by saying, "Now look, when you became a believer you received all of the Holy Spirit you needed."

"Well I'm not going to argue about it, Marilyn. I just know that God has come close to me in a new way and I feel filled to overflowing with His love," he replied.

I decided it was best not to talk about it but over the next fortnight I observed a real change in him. His trust in God grew deeper and he seemed to understand a lot more of the Bible. A new gentleness and love flowed from him.

A crowd from the Christian Union decided to go to hear Jean Darnall preach in a local church. Jean and her husband Elmer are American, but live in this country and run the Christian Life Bible College in London. Due to the teaching I had received I was not in favour of ladies preaching, but David urged me to go. He said that this lady was really filled with the Holy Spirit and had a lot to teach us. Reluctantly I agreed as long as he promised that if I didn't like it he would take me out, because I didn't want to be a captive audience.

We went along to the meeting and Jean Darnall didn't

preach or shout - rather, she seemed to talk to me. Jesus became alive to us all and there was a depth in her words which made me want to have the kind of relationship with Jesus that she was talking about. At the end I went forward, along with a few others, to be prayed for. She prayed for us individually and asked that each one would be filled with God's Holy Spirit. As far as I was concerned nothing happened and I went home feeling frustrated and disillusioned. Why couldn't I speak in this new language? Why didn't I have this bubbling joy? What was wrong with me?

I went through a few months of searching and intense spiritual anguish, wondering why I could not experience what so many of the others had. In the end a friend said to me, "Marilyn, you've got to be much more simple about all this. The baptism of the Holy Spirit is not an experience. It's coming into a closer, deeper relationship with God and being filled more and more with Himself." She pointed me to Luke's Gospel chapter 11, verse 13. The previous verses talk about what a good father is like: if a son asked his father for bread, he wouldn't give him a stone. Then the passage says, "If you then though you are evil (or human) know how to give good gifts to your children, how much more will your Father in heaven give the Holy Spirit to those who ask Him!"

I thought, "Well, I've asked and nothing's happened". I had heard a lot of weird talk about this new prayer language and it had been suggested that maybe these tongues were not from God but from the devil. But I read that passage again, taking note of the different analogies it uses: "If a child asks his father for a fish, he won't give him a snake." Of course not, the father loves his child. I wondered if there was some deep sin in my life which was blocking my receiving more of the Spirit but in the end I realised what God was saying to me: "Be simple when you come to me, just believe and thank Me that I am giving you what you've asked for. Relax and receive it."

So I prayed quietly in my room and said, "Lord, I want to receive all that You have for me - Your Holy Spirit in all His fullness - and I dedicate my life afresh to You". Nothing dramatic happened and I didn't speak in tongues, but as I began to accept that God had heard my prayer and was doing what I had asked, a deep joy, peace and real assurance began to fill my heart.

A few days later I went to a Christian conference led by Jean Darnall at Post Green in Dorset. It was called *Youth Roll-In*, which I thought sounded very American. A girl asked if I had ever spoken in tongues.

"No I haven't," I replied.

"Just go and ask God for it then," she told me. "You don't need to worry about it taking you over. You'll find that your spirit is speaking to God direct, but you'll have full control over it. All you have to do is open your mouth and start praising God."

It sounded too simple, but I decided to try. The only place that was quiet and available at the *Youth Roll-In* conference was the loo, so that's where I prayed! It was there that God gave me my new prayer language.

It sounded a bit like Italian to me so I thought perhaps I was making it up - talk about Doubting Thomas! I do not recommend the course of action I took next. I thought, "Well if it sounded like Italian, maybe I should make it sound more like French next time." But I couldn't - instead it sounded more like double dutch. The new language, on the other hand, was real and had structure and expression, yet I was speaking it with no apparent effort - it was amazing. I kept thinking, "I must be making this up, and anyway what's the point of it if I don't understand what I'm praying?" We are so used to trying to understand everything with our minds that it is difficult for us to adapt when we can't do this. But St. Paul, the greatest missionary, says that we must pray both with our understanding and also with our spirit.

The first time I had an inkling of the kind of power this

prayer language had was when I had a serious argument with someone. There seemed to be no reconciliation between us. Feeling very sad I went quietly away and not knowing what else to do, I prayed in my new language. The person came to see me later and apologised in a way I had never heard from him before. I was amazed and we patched up our differences.

This wonderful prayer language also strengthens and builds us up. When I feel depressed, or I don't feel like praying in the normal way, I can use it and know that I am praying according to God's will. When friends are distressed and I don't know how to pray for them, I use this language and I know that God is enabling me to pray according to what He wants for them.

When I received the Baptism of the Holy Spirit, not only did it give me a new understanding of prayer, it also meant that I came to enjoy reading the Bible much more. This deeper sense of God's presence with me meant that the Christian life was no longer a set of rules to be followed. I found that I wanted to obey Jesus because I loved Him.

I was doing the performers course rather than the degree course at R.C.M. and found the piano technically more difficult than the oboe. With an oboe there is a single line melody to remember, but with the piano there are two hands to put together, which means that memorising the music is much slower. Also because I didn't have many braille textbooks, the history part of the course was difficult to learn.

Jean's friend Beryl, who was the Head of Music at Watford Girls Grammar School, told me that at the end of the year the school were going to lose their oboe teacher. She thought me capable of doing the job, but I couldn't be employed unless I had a teaching diploma. I was thinking of taking the A.R.C.M. - Associate of the Royal College of Music's teaching diploma - in my third year, not my first, but Jean and Beryl thought I could do it earlier. When I broached the subject with my professors at college they had grave doubts, but as Jean and Beryl said, if I didn't give it a try I would never know. So I rose to the challenge and thrust myself wholeheartedly into preparing for the oboe teaching diploma at the end of the first year. To my delight and surprise I passed.

So at the beginning of my second year I started teaching oboe at Watford Girls Grammar School one afternoon a week. It was a wonderful opening but to begin with I needed a lot of help from Beryl and Jean. I didn't know what to do for my first lesson so Jean took the role of a pupil and I practised on her. She also found suitable pieces for me to give the girls and put music into braille for me. (Nowadays the R.N.I.B. have computerised techniques for doing this.)

Jean also taught me the way to the school. There was one difficult part where I had to use a local train and the doors needed to be opened manually. It didn't always arrive at the same platform so if there was no-one else in the carriage I had to open a door and shout to check that I was getting out on the right side. Sometimes if I got no response I leaned down with my stick to feel if the platform was there. Fortunately I never made a mistake!

At first Beryl met me at the school gate and took me to the music room, but eventually I managed to find my own way. Because I was so enthusiastic the first lesson went well over the allotted time. Parents must have got annoyed that week, because their children were late home from school!

A particular problem I had was in not being able to recognise pupil's voices straightaway. Children of eleven or twelve often sound similar and it took me some time before I could recognise some of them. I was all right if I knew the order they were to come in, but otherwise I had to be on my guard. One day - using a much rehearsed diplomatic speech - after carefully explaining to a pupil why she could not go in for a particular exam, I realised that I had been talking to the wrong girl!

Most of my teaching was by example. If I wanted pupils to learn a lip position or fingering, I demonstrated. At first I was embarrassed about touching them to make sure they were standing correctly, but to ensure correct breathing control, posture is very important.

Gradually I managed to overcome the initial hurdles and I found it absolutely thrilling to pass on my knowledge. Teaching, I discovered, was something I thoroughly enjoyed.

# Eight

# Teaching Diploma

Lou Hales was a minister's daughter who was rebelling against the godly lifestyle of home. She had tried to find excitement in the world and had started experimenting with LSD. This had damaged her mind and she often had bad 'trips'. Her life was in a terrible mess and we often prayed for her in the Christian Union because she was known to some of the members.

Lou eventually came to an end of herself and in great distress 'phoned a Christian friend. This girl went to talk and pray with her and as a result Lou gave her life to Christ and moved in with a Christian family. The change in her life was dramatic and she took every opportunity to tell students what had happened to her. She would invite them into the canteen to chat about her Christian faith and the wonderful difference that was becoming so evident in her life.

It was a hard time for her though, because the use of drugs and her former lifestyle had left deep scars in her life which God gradually dealt with. One day I found Lou sitting at the piano in a music room singing. The song was about her relationship with Jesus and expressed her joy at the reality of the relationship she had come into. It sent shivers down my spine.

"It's absolutely fantastic," I said. When she told me she had written it herself and that she had asked the Holy Spirit to help her have the ideas, it set my mind reeling. It had not occurred to me that music could be such a powerful medium for expressing one's faith. I had often thought about being a composer and had tried to write a few songs. My tutor said that I had some gift in composition but my melodies were rather boring, and I knew this was true.

The Christian Union had been asked to lead a youth club meeting the following weekend. We would normally sing classical songs but I thought, "Goodness, these young people aren't going to appreciate that kind of stuff. Maybe we ought to think of doing something more modern." As I didn't know any songs which were suitable, I had an urge to write something myself. I had tried to compose songs before but they had never been very interesting so that evening I prayed earnestly: "Lord, if You can help Lou to write songs as she does, then I believe You can help me in the same way. Please put new ideas and inspiration into my mind. Fill my imagination with Your thoughts and Your words."

Little did I know what this prayer was going to lead to! Nothing seemed to happen at the time but later that week I came up with a song - the very first gospel song I ever wrote: *He's my Saviour, my Friend and my Lord*. I was a bit shy about sharing it with the others at first, partly because I've got such a low voice and had always avoided singing solo. I had been in the choir at school, but I would never do solo parts because I was embarrassed at being unable to hit the high notes. When I did sing the song for the others I was surprised that they really liked it.

We formed a group and had a great time practising in the music room. I decided to sing this song in the youth club meeting. It went down very well so we included it on every other occasion when we went out. We did not stick to the set parts, but improvised as we went along. In the meantime Lou wrote more songs and eventually she got a group together. I loved the words they sang, which were simple but meaningful. Lou was a real inspiration to me and I often sat taping her singing.

After I had spent a year at Harrington Gardens, the owner decided that having a blind person at the hostel was not good for trade and felt it would be better if I left. Miss Banks was quite upset. Even though she was a Jewess, we used to have interesting talks about Jesus and we would discuss Bible passages together. She kept telling the Greek owner that I was no trouble, but I felt it better not to stay where I was not really wanted so I started to hunt for accommodation again, even though it meant that I would have to learn a new route to the college. One of my friends suggested that I went to live in a convent in Kensington Square where they put up quite a few students. At first the idea appalled me. I had never had anything to do with convents or nuns and when I came across their rules I was put off even more. No girls were allowed to wear trousers at dinner time and if anyone was out later than ten o'clock in the evening then she had to stay in one night to make up for it. Being late three times in a row meant expulsion from the convent. I thought, "Oh well, it looks like I'm going to get expelled after one week". I accepted a place with some trepidation.

My parents wondered what on earth it was going to be like as well, but when we arrived at the Convent of the Assumption, we were given a very warm welcome. The nuns were courteous and loving. The accommodation was more spacious than in Harrington Gardens and all the students seemed happy.

Everything seemed free and easy and it was explained that the rules which had worried me no longer applied - they had just not been updated. There was an all-night porter at the door to let students in at whatever time they liked.

My not being a Catholic didn't make any difference - to them at least! There was a girl called Lesley who spoke with a broad Yorkshire accent. She was very good fun and when I first arrived she commented that I seemed to stand to attention every time a nun appeared on the scene! I said it was because I really didn't know how to speak to them and she replied, "OO I don' knoo, they're jus' ordinaree, aren't thee?"

I met some lovely Brazilian friends - Lourdes was the cleaner and her friend Maria Olivia worked in the laundry. I spent many hours with them discussing all sorts of topics and singing with them. When Lourdes saw me she would put her arms around me and give me a great big hug. She was always excited to see me. Maria Olivia was quieter, more of a philosopher, and we had many deep discussions.

When she was young she had contracted polio and Lourdes used to help look after her when her legs became weak. They had been good friends for many years and still live at the convent. One of the nuns, Sister Jo, had played for Victor Sylvester's dance orchestra when younger. She was very interested in my oboe playing and sometimes accompanied me on the piano, But I'm sure we didn't play with quite the swing Victor Sylvester did!

My trips to and from the college weren't as daunting as I had expected because fellow students offered to help me. I was also fortunate in soon making friends with the girls at the convent and I learnt my way round quite quickly. Sue and Sally were particularly helpful. They often put butter and marmalade on my breakfast toast, as spreading evenly is difficult for blind people to do.

In our third year at the College, Sally and I shared a room. The fact that she had *asked* me to be her room mate was an encouragement, because I still had the feeling that sighted people would not want to become too involved with me. Sue was thinking of becoming a Catholic and Sally was interested in religion, so the three of us had a great time talking and discussing various matters. Sally always supported me, but I knew that she wasn't a Christian and I often prayed that she would accept Jesus into her own life. I was thrilled to learn later that she had done so, and she is now not only a good friend, but also a prayer partner in our work.

David and I had been seeing each other regularly and

we started to talk about marriage. When my parents met him they really liked him and I think they held out great hopes for our future. I went to stay with his parents in Chelmsford and initially, because I wasn't on familiar territory, must have given them a negative impression of what a blind person could do. It wasn't easy for them to think of me as a future daughter-in-law but once we got to know each other better they accepted me.

Mum and Dad encouraged us but even though I loved David as a friend I knew deep down that I didn't care for him enough to marry him. In the end by mutual consent we agreed to end our relationship. It was very difficult for a few days after we had finished. It wasn't that I was broken-hearted, it was more that I felt lonely as we had been such close friends and enjoyed doing things together. When David started going out with someone else almost straightaway I found that painful.

After about five or six weeks there was a special service for members of the Christian Union. The speaker was talking about relationships and how we had to care for one another. Afterwards David came and apologised to me for any hurt that he had caused. I said that I was sorry about any pain that I had caused him and from that time on it was great - we continued having lunches together and remained really good friends. In fact, some people thought that we were going out together again.

Sometimes I am asked if I ever regret the decision I made. I don't because I knew that although we were good friends, we were not right for each other. David is now happily married with a family and we still keep in touch occasionally.

Not long after David and I had broken off our relationship I was travelling to Hounslow to visit a blind friend and I had to change trains. I got chatting to a Persian student and it turned out that he went to a college not far from mine. We were getting on well and he seemed charming, helping me to change platforms and waiting with me until my train arrived. Just as he was about to go, he said, "Have you got a boyfriend?"

I replied cheerfully, "No, not at the moment".

"Well would you like to be my girlfriend?" he asked.

On an impulse I said yes. For an instant I felt slightly uneasy but the novelty outweighed any sense of foreboding and I gave him my address. I told him not to use the door near the chapel because there was a special service between 5 and 5.30, the time he said he would pick me up the next day. By the time I arrived at my friend's I was feeling quite worried - how could I have been so naive? I told her the story and she pointed out that as I was a Christian, my values were bound to be different from his. The trouble was that I had arranged to meet him and I did not know how to get out of the situation, so I just prayed that he wouldn't turn up!

At about 5.25 the next day, there was a loud knock on the door near the chapel and a lot of scurrying around as people went to see what the disturbance was about. The common room door opened and one of the assistants said, "Marilyn, there's a lovely young man waiting here for you". He came into the room and before I could do anything he had swept me into his arms and given me an extremely passionate kiss.

"Hello, my darling," he said. "I've been looking forward to this evening so much."

I was somewhat taken aback and didn't know what to do.

"I thought I could take you to my flat darling, where we could play records and have a nice evening together."

I felt extremely uncomfortable and knew my face turned red as I said, "No, I'm sorry but I've made rather a mistake. I shouldn't have agreed to see you."

"What do you mean my darling?" he queried.

"I want you to know that it has nothing to do with colour prejudice, but I'm afraid I've changed my mind and

I don't think we can go out together," I replied.

"But why on earth not? You said you would like to be my girlfriend." And he proceeded to give me another passionate kiss.

"Please let me explain," I said. "I'm a Christian and I think that my understanding of a nice evening is rather different from yours. For a start, I don't believe in sex outside marriage."

"Everyone's the same these days," he said. "All religions mix together and you've got to have sex. It doesn't matter now. I mean everybody has it. It's like taking exercise." He wasn't taking me seriously.

"Well not for me it isn't," I replied, backing away.

"You know you can't do without it. Ninety nine per cent of girls have it."

"I'm just one of the one per cent then that doesn't."

"But my darling, relax and enjoy yourself. You just don't understand these things and I will make it such a lovely evening for you."

"I'm sorry to disappoint you, but I'm afraid I just cannot come with you," I said. He embraced me again passionately and I withdrew before adding, "Well I'm sorry, but I've got to say goodbye."

"Can't I possibly persuade you my darling?"

"No."

"Well goodbye and I certainly am very disappointed," he said.

"It's all my fault and I hope you won't take it the wrong way," I muttered as he stumped out of the room. I breathed a sigh of relief but I had certainly learnt my lesson.

On the day of my twenty first birthday I was at the Royal College of Music and my friends arranged a party for me. A minister of a local church had offered to lend us some plates and cutlery for the occasion. He told me to ring him on the afternoon of the party but I could not get through on the 'phone. I tried for an hour and a half and went upstairs in despair wondering what on earth people were going to put food on. (It didn't occur to me to use paper plates!) I was halfway up the stairs when I suddenly heard a man say to me, "Try again". I whirled round, not recognising the voice.

"Pardon?" I said but there was no reply. There was no-one there but I was sure somebody had spoken to me. I stood still wondering what to make of it. Suddenly I realised it must have been either God or an angel talking to me. So I went back to the phone and rang the number again. I could hardly believe it when I got through straightaway. It was incredible. As a result we were able to get the plates and cutlery for my party, which was a great success. What happened that day is a wonderful example of how God is interested in the most mundane things that we do. We often try to separate secular and spiritual things, but God loves us to enjoy ourselves and He wanted that occasion to be special for me - and it certainly was.

Mum and Dad put on another coming of age party for me at home during the holidays. Mum made lots of food, especially things she knew I liked. I particularly remember a trifle which was fantastic. Both friends and relatives were invited and my Auntie Marjorie, of whom I was very fond, got a bit merry! The party really did go with a swing. My parents had gone to a lot of trouble to make this celebration memorable for me.

At the end of my second year of college I took my piano teacher's diploma, which I found a real struggle. Jean Coates helped me a great deal because my own teachers were ill part of the time and my lessons interrupted. I was then offered the chance of some teaching at Chorleywood College. The piano teacher, who was blind herself, had reached retirement age and Jean offered me the job.

It wasn't easy going back to my old school as a teacher so soon after leaving. I was now equal to those who had taught me and it was particularly difficult because some of my friends were still students! I was ill at ease in the staff room and never quite felt like a fully fledged teacher. Later on I was offered more work at the Girls Grammar School so I was teaching three times a week in the Watford/Chorleywood area.

I was recommended by the RCM to teach a young singer to play the oboe. Not knowing much about pop music I didn't recognise Peter Gabriel as a member of the well-known group Genesis. When I mentioned Peter to the girls at the grammar school they almost swooned and I definitely went up in their estimation!

In the third year I worked for the Licentiate of the Royal Academy of Music performers' diploma on the oboe. It was the highest diploma I could attain and both difficult and time-consuming. My examiner was the famous oboist Evelyn Rothwell and I felt it a real honour to play in front of her. She was quite a hard examiner and had very high standards. Even though I didn't play my best, probably because I was nervous, I did pass. I was offered the chance of doing a fourth year of studies at college but I was enjoying teaching so much that I declined the offer, as I wanted to show others how to appreciate and play music.

At the end of three happy years as a student it was time for me to move on. I had learnt a lot about music but also about coping with life as a blind person in a world of sighted people, and I had proved I could manage to live independently. Even more important, I had experienced the love of the God who had cared and provided for me in so many ways. During those years my Christian faith had grown in leaps and bounds as I learnt more about God's love and His character.

# Nine

# Earning a Living

I now had the necessary diplomas - L.R.A.M. and A.R.C.M. - but what was the next step? What would the future hold? Where would I live? Now that I was no longer a student I would need to earn a living. The obvious thing seemed to be to live near Watford or Chorleywood which was where I was getting work. Mum and Dad decided that they would try to buy me a house. They had apparently been thinking for a long time that it was important for me to be independent and not to have to rely on rented accommodation, which would not be as secure as having my own property.

I really valued their sacrifice in taking on such a big financial commitment for me. They searched for a house around the Watford area during the weekends and lived in their caravan, which meant that they could move around and not have the expense of staying in hotels.

In 1972 house prices were really rocketing and down south they were much higher than in the Birmingham area. I prayed a great deal about their choice of house because I wanted to be in the place where God wanted me. I knew that He had a plan for my life and that my location was important to Him. I trusted my parents' judgement in choosing a suitable house, knowing that they would understand what I needed.

As I had decided that I wanted to share with someone else, the house needed at least two bedrooms. For convenience there had to be a shop nearby and of course it needed to be near a good bus route.

Mum and Dad had been looking for quite a while and I began to feel that they might not find a suitable place before the start of the new teaching term. The convent agreed that I could stay there and commute if it became necessary, but fortunately it didn't.

On the last day of my college term, Mum and Dad picked me up from the convent. I said a fond goodbye to all my friends before getting into the car for the drive home to Birmingham.

Dad said, "We have found you a house and we've made an offer for it. It's £11,500." That was a lot of money in the early seventies and they could have got a similar house for half the price in Birmingham. Before putting in the offer Dad had said to Mum, "We'll never see that money back, Marion". They really wondered if they had done the right thing.

Their offer was accepted and I suddenly felt a great sense of excitement and responsibility now that I was to become the owner of my own property. It was the beginning of September when I took my first look at the house. Mum and Dad waited with baited breath as I walked into the hall and went through all the rooms. I loved it straightaway. I sensed that it was just the right house for me and I'm still living in my modest but lovely home. It has two bedrooms, a big lounge and dining room combined and a hatch, or bar as we called it, through to a small kitchen.

Then came the challenge and fun of creating a new home. Mum and Dad stayed with me and there seemed a lot to do, buying furniture and mundane things like tea towels, dishcloths and wastepaper bins. For my twenty first birthday, several people had bought me items for the home which I had asked for, knowing that setting up house was a possibility, but even so I still needed a lot more. Mum and Dad worked very hard to help me. We went to Woolworths to get some furniture and they gave me money to spend. Fortunately Dad was a handyman and among other things he assembled a cocktail cabinet. Mum and Dad had just bought themselves a new lounge suite. As their old one was quite small it fitted into my house nicely, so they had it re-upholstered to fit in with the colour scheme. Mum made curtains and soon the new house became a real home.

Dad had to return to Birmingham because of the business, but Mum stayed on for a few weeks to help me learn the routes around the neighbourhood. It must have been a very traumatic time for her because she was wondering how I would manage on my own. There were so many things to learn and Mum was probably more aware of them than I was.

It was a complicated route to and from the Girls Grammar School. I had to travel by bus, train and on foot and Mum came with me several times. When I had mastered the route and came home alone in the evening I appreciated knowing that she was there waiting for me. She usually had a cooked meal ready, and the opportunity to be together and share in this new experience was good for us both.

I started going to St. James Road Baptist Church and it was arranged for Margaret and John Hughes, members of the congregation, to collect me on Sundays. Although the church services were much quieter than I was used to I found the people made me most welcome. I went along to the youth meeting on the first Sunday night and sat next to a girl called Hilary. I had been told that she was looking for accommodation, but she seemed very quiet and I thought she wouldn't be 'my cup of tea' because I like people to be chatty. As it turned out she was just rather shy. We met again the next week and I asked if she would be interested in looking at my house with a view to sharing it with me. Hilary came round and we had a coffee together and chatted. Apparently she had never met a blind person before, but she seemed a very gentle, warm person. Before she left we prayed together about whether or not she should move in and she said she would give me her decision in a week's time. I thought this a lovely way to end our meeting and felt an assurance that she was the right person. Waiting the week for her decision felt more like a month but when she said the answer was yes I was delighted and relieved. Hilary moved in at the beginning of October and I enjoyed sharing the house with her.

Initially I tried to have a meal ready when she came in from her work at the Scripture Union Bookshop in London. She must have been rather tired of having burnt potatoes or dried-up chips, so one evening at the end of the week she quietly suggested that she should do some of the cooking! Hilary had a deep faith and taught me a great deal about how to show God's love to people in practical ways. She was the kind of person who could always see when people were in need or lonely, and would invite them home for a meal. Sometimes this frustrated me because we never had a quiet Sunday on our own. But she was unstinting in her giving, and a very selfless kind of person. As she had been in the church for a long time she helped me get to know a lot of people.

We discovered that we had a lot in common and became the best of buddies. Our friendship developed into one of the deepest of my life and I was constantly amazed that God had brought us together and that Hilary genuinely enjoyed my company.

Hilary and I went to a weekly housegroup meeting where we learnt more about the gifts and power of the Holy Spirit. We also discovered more about worship and the constancy of God's love. He loved us just the same no matter how we felt - whether we had had a good day or a bad day. We learnt not to be inward-looking or feel condemned if things had gone wrong and I found the teaching at these meetings enabled me to centre my mind upon my Heavenly Father and all He could do for me, rather than focusing on my own problems.

I was thrilled with owning my own house, and I can never thank Mum and Dad enough for what they did in buying it for me. Having helpful next door neighbours was a great bonus. Phyllis and Jack Chapel were a joy to know and helped with the small garden and other odd jobs. I couldn't have chosen to live next to nicer people and Mum and Dad felt happier knowing they were there to keep an eye on me!

Not long after moving into my new home I decided that a guide dog would be a great help to me. It was something I had thought about for a while and many of my friends said how much their dogs took the strain out of walking along busy streets. Using a stick took a lot of concentration.

I found school corridors particularly awkward, and thought a dog would be able to negotiate a way more easily through the throngs of children. Another advantage would be that as most children like animals, pupils would relax more when they came for lessons. So I wrote to the Guide Dogs for the Blind Association and a trainer was sent to assess me. He walked around the street and I had to hold the harness and pretend that he was the dog. (Matching the dog's build and temperament with its owner's is vitally important if the partnership is to work properly). There was a waiting list for trained dogs so I managed as best I could in the meantime. At Christmas, I had notification from the Guide Dog Centre to say that if I wanted a dog urgently I would have to go to Forfar in Scotland where a suitable dog was available. I was amazed that I had heard from them so soon.

A short while later I took the long journey to Forfar feeling quite apprehensive, because I had never had much to do with animals. As a child I had often had nightmares about snappy little dogs hanging around my heels! At Forfar I met my trainer Bill Logan and two days later we were introduced to our dogs. There were several of us in the group and we were all excited at the prospect. Mine was an adorable little black labrador called Susie and I felt very proud of her. She was extremely quiet - almost *too* quiet and placid, I thought.

At the newly equipped training centre there was underfloor central heating and my first problem in handling Susie arose on the first night. Once allocated, our dogs remained with us all the time so that we could build up a relationship with them. They were supposed to spend the night on their beds in our rooms - Susie would not! She was determined to lie on the warm floor under my bed and she just wouldn't get up in the morning. Not being used to handling dogs I got more and more desperate. Knowing that I was late for breakfast I sometimes had to resort to getting under the bed and pulling her out by the leg - not to be recommended! I tried to explain this to the trainers but I must admit it did sound rather feeble when they said, "You're late Miss Baker," and I replied, "I'm afraid it was the dog. She wouldn't get up." Susie was very sensitive and excellent at her work, but I found the training sessions quite difficult - mainly because of my lack of good directional sense. It was also strange being amongst so many blind people again!

I stayed at Forfar for a month and met some lovely Christians whom the Bannard-Smiths put me in touch with. One day I sat in John and Helen Meyer's lounge and tried to play the bagpipes. It was a tremendous experience but I could hardly believe how hard it was to produce a note - though I did manage it in the end. I was shocked at how loud they sounded and realised that's why bagpipes are usually played outside!

After a hard working month Susie and I went home to Watford. Mum and Dad met us off the train. I was feeling very proud of Susie, who had successfully brought me home safely - it was the first time we had been a completely independent team and I wanted to show her off. Dad surprised me with the remark, "Goodness, Susie looks frail. I wouldn't have thought her strong enough to be a guide dog."

Over the next month Susie was a tremendous help to me. Routes that I had not been able to attempt before with a white stick, I now managed to do with Susie and I thought her the best guide dog in the world. I had to get other people to walk the route with us first so that Susie wouldn't learn it wrongly. One day somebody asked me, "How does your dog know which tube train to get onto?" I laughed and said, "I have to ask somebody, of course".

It was amazing the difference a guide dog made not only with regard to my independence but in relation to other people: in the streets people came up to talk to me and most of my pupils loved her.

As well as teaching oboe and piano, I was also now teaching clarinet at the Girls Grammar School and was agreeably surprised when the headmaster from the Boys Grammar School rang me to ask if I was able to do some wind instrument teaching there. I was glad to take such a marvellous opportunity especially as it was only a short walk from my home.

Duncan, who attended the Boys Grammar School, adored dogs. His dad was a butcher and one day Duncan brought a huge bone in for Susie. He begged me to give it to her during the lesson. I was reluctant at first but in the end I unwrapped it and she began to munch it on the cold stone floor of the music room. The lesson took place with this rather new kind of percussion, but then to my horror the Head of Music walked in. This was very unusual and I didn't really know what to do as I hadn't been teaching at the school long. I bent down and tried to gather up the bone quickly, pretending that my dog had somehow got it out of the bag herself. Fortunately he was very friendly and didn't seem to notice anything unusual about a dog eating a bone in a music lesson! Teachers at all the schools were helpful and Susie was almost accepted as part of the staff.

Muriel and I had kept contact with each other and she

was still determined to make me into a confident cook, so she invited me to stay with her in Lincoln for a weekend. Susie and I went on the train together and we had a wonderful time. From eight o'clock in the morning until seven o'clock at night we were in the kitchen cooking all sorts of different dishes. She had thoughtfully devised many different ways of helping me to get over cooking difficulties. For instance I loved fried eggs, but because of the problem of finding them in the pan and getting them out in one piece, I had given up cooking them. Muriel's method was to use a metal pastry cutter. First I melted the fat in the pan and when it sizzled I placed the pastry cutter in the centre and broke the egg into it. I tested it with my finger to see if it was done and found to my surprise that it was not too hot to touch. Then, with the oven glove over my hand, I lifted both pastry cutter and egg out of the pan.

Muriel also showed me how to peel vegetables while they were under warm water, because in that way it is easier to feel whether the skin has all been removed. I had a problem when making cakes in that I used to leave a lot of mixture at the bottom of the bowl but Muriel taught me how to go round it systematically with a plastic spatula so that I got virtually all the mixture out. She assured me that many of the best chefs used their fingers more than the average cook, so she encouraged me to do the same and it did make a great deal of difference.

For me the crowning glory of the 'Cordon Bleu' cookery course was the black forest gateau. A group of friends came in the evening to eat the delights we had prepared and I could hardly believe what I had achieved. The food tasted superb!

As a result of this time with Muriel I now enjoy cooking, especially savoury dishes like casseroles, using lots of herbs and garlic. Decorating cakes and doing fiddly things is not my forté. Muriel really believed in me and I realised that with a little thought and effort I could achieve good results. Now cooking is one of my favourite hobbies. I particularly enjoy bread-making - so my name does suit! There is nothing nicer than getting up early in the morning and making a batch of rolls for breakfast. Maybe that's because I like the fact that a small piece of dough rises into something much bigger. It seems good economy to me!

At school I ate the meals provided in the dining room but this was a place that Susie hated. She crawled under the table and started to tremble. At first I thought she was just being silly so wasn't too concerned, but as the months went by Susie began to get more and more withdrawn. She would hide herself upstairs and sit behind the door in the bathroom at home. Often I found her there trembling with her head down. She still had the habit of not wanting to get up in the morning and instead of running when I got out her lead as other dogs did, she hid. It was hard to get her from under the beds and it wasn't because of underfloor central heating this time! The trainer came to make the normal six monthly check, and I spoke with concern about Susie's nervousness. He thought that she was just rather sensitive and would soon settle down, but unfortunately she didn't.

She became very frightened when it thundered and lightened. Once I hit my head on a post outside a fish and chip shop because she had been so startled by a thunder clap. The owner invited me in and gave me a cup of tea before taking me home. After a bad thunder storm Susie would be off her food for at least two days. I realised it was getting to the point where any loud noise upset her. The vet called it 'noise shyness'. I began to notice the sounds which upset her and I became jumpy too, which I'm sure didn't help. Even wind in the chimney at home frightened her and on Bonfire Night she was absolutely terrified.

Sometimes she seemed to enjoy her work, but at other

times she would go so slowly that I'd be late for lessons. This used to make me frustrated and sometimes I would smack her because she seemed so stubborn. Again, in desperation I took her to the local vet who said that she was under grave strain and put her on a sedative. I rang up Leamington Spa Guide Dogs Training Centre, whose care I was under, and told them about her symptoms. One of the head trainers came to see her and after talking with me and observing Susie, we agreed that she would have to give up work - after only eighteen months. It was with a sad heart that I had to accept this. My father had been right - she just wasn't strong enough to cope. To guide me through the busy streets of Watford had been too much for her, having come from a much quieter environment. Susie went to live with Doris, who was the captain of the Girls Brigade in my church. I had recently become an officer in the Brigade myself so we knew each other well. Susie was very fond of Doris and settled happily with her. Eventually they moved to Guildford together. The more relaxed, peaceful way of life suited Susie well and she lived to a ripe old age.

When Susie went the house seemed empty and I missed her company very much. We had gone through so much together. Fortunately I only had a few days to wait before going to Leamington Spa for a replacement but I knew that even though I would have another dog, the relationship would never be the same as I had had with Susie.

# Ten

# Susie's Replacement

Leamington Spa Training Centre realised that I needed a robust dog with a strong temperament because of the busy life I led and the next dog chosen for me was Yuma, who was a complete contrast to Susie. She was a golden labrador retriever cross who was extremely boisterous, very greedy, very intelligent and quite noisy - a yellow ball of fun. Instead of walking, she pulled and I often found myself running behind her. She took a great deal of taming down! When I got her home to Watford Hilary was frightened of her and it was a big shock to have such a lively animal around the house after gentle Susie.

If I ever went out and left Yuma she hated it and everyone knew! Once she chewed up some of the clarinet reeds and an expensive microphone. When I took her to Sainsbury's I would tie her up by the check-out while I went around the store with an assistant to get my shopping. Yuma used to make such a noise that all sorts of people came up to her and stroked her. In the end it got so embarrassing that I took her round the supermarket with me. Walking through the aisles laden with food was a great temptation to her and I was never sure what she would try to pinch! There was nothing that Yuma didn't want to take - bread from a lady's shopping basket, chocolates from a baby's hand, cakes from the baker, and chops from the butcher. Trifles, gateaux and bread and butter also disappeared from tea trolleys when we were invited out!

She got a dreadful reputation but I loved her and most of the time she was good at her work. I trusted her implicitly. When it snowed one day the paths and roads were covered. Snow to a blind person is like fog to someone sighted. It's easy to lose your sense of direction when sound is deadened and I didn't know where we were, but Yuma did. She stopped at the right kerbs to cross the roads and got us back safely.

I have always been interested in the work of the Torch Trust for the Blind and had read their magazines while a teenager at Chorleywood College. Torch Trust is a Christian organisation putting literature onto cassettes and into braille and large print. Its founders Mr. and Mrs. Heath now act as houseparents to the large family of blind and sighted people who live and work at Torch House in Leicestershire.

At this time they had fellowship groups springing up all over the country and I felt it would be good to start one up in Watford. Through this group Hilary and I met Maureen. She was deaf, nearly blind and epileptic. Maureen had been living in a Rudolf Steiner home, but she had recently moved into a home for the blind in St. Albans. I had never had anything to do with deaf people before and found it difficult to communicate with Maureen. She wore two hearing aids and as her sight was not good, she couldn't lip read very well either. However she was able to understand me when I spoke loudly and distinctly. Sometimes I would spell words onto her hand but that was rather a slow process. Hilary was more able to communicate with Maureen and with her help I got better at it, so Maureen and I soon became close friends.

Although she was handicapped she was very mischievous and when she entered a room everyone knew it! She used to write poetry and one day when I had been messing about with a friend's moped, Maureen presented me with a hilarious poem on the subject. No-one had ever given Maureen any real job to do because they didn't think her capable. She mentioned this to me one day and I made some passing remark about needing someone to help clean the house. She volunteered like a shot and came down by herself from St. Albans on the bus each week to do it. She was very proud of her work and I would find everything spick and span when I got home. She was so conscientious that she even managed to get the black non-stick surface off the cooker because she thought it was dirt! She came to stay with us at weekends and we had some really good times together.

When we first got to know Maureen it was only occasionally that she had a fit at our house, but these increased as time went by. In spite of this she became a committee member of our Torch Fellowship Group and did a great deal of work for it, although it was difficult at times to get over to her what was happening at the meetings.

After a fit Maureen felt ill for several hours and as the intensity and frequency of them increased, she became more and more unwell. Often when I returned home from work I would find her huddled in a chair, but we loved having her with us, even though it put a strain on us all.

The hospital increased her drugs, which made her drowsy and unsteady on her feet. Eventually it was decided that she should go to live at a home run by Torch Trust in Sussex so that she would have constant care. Although we kept in touch by tape - if I spoke clearly to her she could understand my voice - it wasn't the same as seeing each other and many times I planned to visit her but circumstances didn't allow it.

One morning before I went to school I received a phone call from Torch Trust to tell me that Maureen had died suddenly. She hadn't felt well that morning and had gone back to bed for a while. When one of the staff took up her breakfast she discovered that Maureen was dead. A severe fit had caused her to have a heart attack. In many ways it was a blessing because she was becoming frustrated by the limitations imposed on her: God had lightened her load. I sang at her funeral and composed a special song just for her. I know that God inspired me to write it and the last verse says:

Maureen now you're in your real home above
Wrapped in God's eternal love.
You're more alive and radiant than you've ever been before.
One day I'll be talking with you there.
Think of all the joys we'll share
With our lovely Jesus evermore.

After Hilary had been with me for three and a half years, she received the tragic news that her brother's wife had been drowned, leaving him with two young children. Hilary came to the conclusion, after a lot of thought and prayer, that it was right for her to go and look after the family. The night before she was planning to tell me, God spoke to me about it Himself.

We had been such close friends for three and a half years that it was going to be a terribly sad time for us both - sad for Hilary because her whole way of life was going to change and sad for me because it was like the bottom of my world falling out. I couldn't imagine life without this gentle, warm-hearted, Christlike person who had become like a sister to me. Because I knew how hard it was going to be for her to tell me, I broached the subject when she brought me a cup of tea in the morning. She was relieved that I had done so and it was confirmation to us both when we realised that the Lord had shown us independently what Hilary should do.

It's truly wonderful though how God plans ahead for us. One of the helpers at the Girls' Brigade, Carol Franklin, was studying at London Bible College and lived in rooms there. Hilary suggested that I ask her to come and live in the house, but I wasn't sure as she seemed even shyer than Hilary had been when we first met. In the end Hilary mentioned the possibility to Carol one evening after Girls' Brigade. I went out of the room while they talked together because I still found it difficult to accept Hilary's leaving.

Carol told Hilary that on the 'Quiet Day' at the College the previous month she had gone for a walk to think and pray. God had spoken to her clearly and had said that He wanted her to come and live with me. But time had passed and she thought she must have been mistaken, because I had not asked her to do so. When I returned to the room and was told this I was really amazed at how God had prepared Carol's heart. He had wonderfully provided for my needs and Carol moved in with me just after Easter 1976.

Doris, who took Susie to Guildford to live, gave us her little Fiat 500 before moving and Carol and I had great fun with it. One night just after Carol moved in, it broke down and we had to push it home at about midnight. That same weekend Carol locked herself out of the house and I wondered what kind of a lifestyle we were going to enjoy together! But fortunately we became firm friends.

Carol was very musical even though she had never been to music college and because of our mutual interest, my Christian musical career really began at that time. Although I had written one successful song at the RCM I had not written anything else since. I don't really know why - maybe it was because I was busy with exams and getting to grips with teaching, and then when Hilary came along, life was full as we enjoyed entertaining at home. But now in the evenings Carol and I would make music together. She would sing her favourite songs while I played the piano. She sang with such simplicity and her voice, though untrained, had a lovely pure quality. It was through these times that a deep urge was awakened in me to write songs again. I began with choruses which I wrote for her to sing while I accompanied her.

She took some singing lessons and we prayed that if God wanted us to use these songs further He would open up opportunities. Out of the blue, our minister Richard Harbour rang us up one day and asked "Would you and Carol like to do something in our next communion service?"

"What do you mean, do something?" I replied.

"Well Carol could sing and you could play for her."

"Did you know that Carol is taking singing lessons?" I asked.

"No," he replied, "I just thought that I'd like you to try and do something together".

So we agreed. Our first song was called *My Love Will Never Fail You* and afterwards people came up and told us how beautiful the words were and how helpful they had found it. So I wrote others. I didn't think about writing them for me to sing, but sometimes I sang a harmony underneath.

Geoffrey Yates, who worked for Christian Audio Visual Services, came to the church to look at the public address system. He heard Carol and me and suggested, somewhat to our surprise, that we make a record together.

I was reminded of a prophecy given to me months earlier. When Hilary and I had been attending the housegroup meetings and learning how to draw closer to God someone from Northern Ireland had been speaking one evening. After he had finished he came round to talk to each one of us personally, explaining that God often gave him the gift of encouraging people into what He wanted them to do in the future.

When he came to me, he said that God had chosen me to be a musical missionary. I was quite amazed. The speaker went on to say that I would be going not only to this country but to other nations and that my music would be a great encouragement and help to many people. You can imagine how strange this sounded at the time, because I had not made any records or even written many songs. In fact the whole thing had sounded so incredible that I had forgotten about it and only recalled it when Geoffrey made his suggestion.

Carol and I agreed to give it a try and Geoffrey brought the recording equipment around to our house. The album consisted mainly of piano playing. Printed words were included and the idea was that listeners could sing along with the record to well-known choruses. We also included a few songs I had written which Carol and I sang together and I sang one called *Love* on my own. The words had been written by my friend Maureen a few months before she died. When I played her the song, although she couldn't hear it very well, she had tears in her eyes because she felt the music expressed the words so graphically. The album was called *Open our Eyes Lord*.

What I hadn't realised beforehand was that I had to *buy* five hundred of these records. When I found out, I was really shocked. "How on earth will I be able to sell that many?" I asked Richard and Shirley Harbour in some alarm. Richard said that he would try and get me invitations to sing at some local churches and women's meetings, which would provide some outlets. But I need not have feared. The album sold very quickly and we soon had to get more records and tapes done.

We heard of some wonderful and interesting incidents from people who had been helped through listening to the songs. One lady said that she had been healed from claustrophobia and many said that the words and music brought deep peace and joy to their hearts. We were amazed and thrilled. Geoffrey wanted us to do another record, but that idea didn't materialise.

During the second year Carol was living with me, we were invited to go to Canada to stay with her Auntie Joan and Uncle Nick in Calgary. It was a tremendous adventure for me and I was very excited about travelling. I had only been abroad once before and that was on a student exchange to France when I was a teenager. It had been a traumatic experience because the girl I stayed with was partially sighted, her mother and father had been divorced and her father was trying to look after the family. I became ill while there, probably because I had eaten too much food that I wasn't used to. We had to call in medical help, which resulted in an expensive doctor's bill.

But that experience was now far behind me and I was greatly looking forward to our holiday in Canada. Mum and I stayed the night at Carol's parents and they drove us to Gatwick for our flight. Yuma went back with Mum to stay in Birmingham while I was away.

Carol's uncle and aunt made us tremendously welcome and gave us a very memorable time. The Canadian way of life was a real eye-opener and totally different from anything I had known before - everything was so much bigger than I was used to. Auntie Joan and Uncle Nick took us camping in the mountains, and we also went to a family holiday camp situated by a beautiful lake. We often ate meals out of doors, usually cooked on a barbeque. Carol and I spent hours on a raft on the water but we didn't realise how hot the sun was. As a result we got badly burnt and urgently needed some medication!

We flew to Vancouver for a few days and stayed with friends connected with our church. While there I handled a speed-boat on my own. It was a wonderful experience to be in control of such a powerful boat and to feel the bumping of the waves as we raced around the harbour.

I made a tape recording of the highlights of the holiday. The commentary included the sound of the speed-boat and the sizzling noise when we cooked food on a barbeque. Obviously blind people cannot get enjoyment from looking at photographs so a tape recording is a good way of reliving happy events.

This holiday though was tinged with sadness because now that Carol had come to the end of her course at Bible College she was going to start work with the Torch Trust. Although she had enjoyed being involved in singing and making the record, she did not feel this was what God wanted her to do on a permanent basis.

When Carol moved out I really missed our times together, both our music sessions and our other shared interests. I met another girl, Marjorie, again through the Girls' Brigade, and as Carol left she came to share my house.

Marjorie and I continued to work in the Girls' Brigade, but after Doris left I found it more difficult to control the girls. Some were very mischievious and it was hard for me to recognise the culprits. They knew this and took advantage of the situation, so I thought it best to leave. I had spent several happy years with the Girls' Brigade, but now I needed more time to spend on my music.

Unlike Carol, Marjorie was not a singer but she used to take me round to sing in different places when she could. She worked shifts as a nurse, so this wasn't always easy. Marjorie was very fond of Yuma and enjoyed having a dog around the house. One day when I was at the Boys Grammar school I let Yuma out for a run but she would not come back. I called and called and sent some of the boys to search for her, but there was no sign. About an hour later, feeling worried and not too sure what to do, I was amazed when Marjorie arrived at the music room door with Yuma. The 'naughty madam', as I called her, had run back home and Marjorie, who had been working nights, was sound asleep when Jack Chapel from next door woke her up with the news that Yuma was standing at our front door. Marjorie, realising what had happened, had got up and dressed and brought Yuma back to the school on a piece of string, since I had the lead. I didn't know whether to give Yuma a hug or a scolding!

# Eleven

# Spiritual Songs

I began to write more songs as I wanted to pour out my heart in music to share with others the amazing love of God. Although many people wouldn't listen to sermons I thought that they might listen to a song, especially if it was a good one, but I realised that I could not write these songs without the help of the Holy Spirit. I was trying to put over the most important message that mankind would ever hear so the songs had to be of the highest calibre - only the very best was good enough for God. I felt that some of the shoddy unprofessional songs which I had heard degraded the Christian message instead of helping it.

Len Magee was pastor of an Elim Church in Watford around that time and had heard the album *Open Our Eyes*. He felt that I should make a different kind of record, on which I would do more of the singing, and encouraged me to get some new material together. Richard and Shirley Harbour also said that they felt this was more than just a pastime or a hobby, and that it could be an important sphere of service which God was opening up to me.

One afternoon, with great trepidation, I went to visit the Managing Director of Marshall Morgan and Scott, who made records under the Pilgrim label. I had sent a demonstration tape and now I sat in David Payne's office in London. He asked me a lot of questions about why I was writing these songs and what I hoped to achieve. At the time, he came over as a hard-headed businessman without much interest in the product. By the end of the interview I didn't think I had got on very well and I was right, because he wasn't very keen to record me. But nevertheless Len Magee, who was a friend of his, persuaded him that it would be worth his giving me a chance to do a record. So because David trusted Len's judgement, he said I could go ahead.

Sue McClennan the producer came to visit me in Watford. She sounded like a lady member of the Beatles with a broad Liverpuddlian accent, and some of the things she said I didn't understand. She called me 'kid' and talked about the 'vibes' in the studio. At first I thought this was short for vibrophone, which could have been an instrument, but later I realised she meant the atmosphere! I sang some of my songs to her because she had lost my demo tape and she exclaimed, "Where did you get these from kid?" When I told her that I had written them, she said, "Yer never - did yer?" Her visit was brief and my mind felt in a daze. I rang Carol to ask if she would be able to come and sing on the record with me, and when she agreed I felt much better, knowing her presence would have a calming effect.

Making my first studio record turned out to be one of the most traumatic experiences in my life. We recorded at The Old Smithy in Worcester, and stayed in a cottage in the grounds. We cooked a meal for breakfast, but after that there was no time to stop, so we lived on take-aways or rolls from the local pub.

Because I had not made a record like this before I didn't know what to expect. Neither did Carol, and we both felt tired and strained. Normally I sang and played at the same time, but now I needed to record the piano parts first and add the voice later. I found this very difficult, because to make the piano part really expressive I felt I needed to sing as well. The other problem was that I kept making mistakes, probably due to nerves. Because the piano is not my first instrument it has never been that easy for me to play. Making the odd mistake in a concert doesn't spoil the whole performance, but mistakes on a record are heard each time it is played and so accuracy is essential.

After a while our nerves were on edge because we sometimes worked from nine o'clock in the morning until one or two o'clock at night. The other players, I felt, didn't come up to the high standards I had been used to at the Royal College. Hired session musicians came to play the guitar and drums but I didn't like the heavy way the drummer played and I found the base player extremely unimaginative. To make matters worse, even though I knew nothing about base playing, I tried to tell him exactly what I wanted by making him write down a part. Sue was furious and shouted, "How dare you tell the base player what to do!" I shouted back that if he had more imagination himself, I wouldn't need to. It was difficult too to keep in time with the drummer because I wasn't used to playing to such a strict beat. I knew he was right and I was the one who varied my timing, but that didn't help.

After about five days of being in the studio, I felt I wanted to quit altogether. I decided that this was the last time I was going to do a record. We were supposed to work as a team but we didn't - the producer and I didn't seem to hit if off and everybody's musical ideas seemed different from mine. We had not prayed together or even mentioned the Lord, which was wrong considering that all the songs were about Him. The situation came to a head when we had been working very late one night. The next morning I was called to the phone early and it was someone from church. I was feeling very drowsy and also tearful and I asked the church to pray very urgently about the recording.

The prayer was answered. Sue came in to our room and sat down. "I've made a mess of all this, haven't I?" she said. "I know these songs are good but I've not produced anything that has needed such a lot of care before."

Carol had been listening and she suggested that we talked to the Lord about it together. Sue was the first to pray: she asked God to forgive her and help her, and told me she was sorry for driving me too hard. I apologised to her and prayed that God would help me to get my parts right and to be more patient. Finally we all prayed that we would work properly together as a team.

It was incredible how the atmosphere changed. Suddenly we began to trust one another and when we made mistakes, we laughed. We still had disagreements about the way the music should be arranged, but the tension had gone. Not only were we working together as a team, but we also became good friends, particularly Sue, Carol and I.

I knew what kind of atmosphere I wanted to produce in the songs, but I wasn't experienced enough in musical arrangement to know what instruments could create it. Sometimes I knew that we hadn't achieved what I had intended in a particular song, but I found it hard to explain why. Sue did go to a lot of trouble to get the songs right but they had been born out of the deepest experiences of my life and when I heard them changed, altered and shaped differently I felt as if part of my very soul was being torn to pieces.

I had heard that where there is a spiritual blessing, there is always a real price to pay. That certainly seemed to be the case with this record, which had taken its toll physically and spiritually. Yet God really anointed the end result and used it in an incredible way.

The record was called *He Gives Joy* and when David Payne heard it, he was thrilled. He rang me and said he hadn't believed it could be so good. Our respect for each other began to grow.

By this time I was teaching in five schools around the Watford area. I was also able to teach private pupils at home as Dad had paid for a new music room to be built on to the back of my house. After the record was released

I began to get more engagements. The record sold amazingly well and I received an increasing number of letters from people who told me that the songs had been a deep source of help and strength to them in times of crisis. I knew the traumatic time in the studio had been worth it.

In the summer after *He Gives Joy* was released I attended a special *Christian and the Arts* week organised at Lee Abbey where Adrian Snell was to lead a songwriting course.

He was unexpectedly called away to attend a funeral and asked me if I would take over. I agreed, but I was quite nervous and didn't sleep much that night. He wanted everyone in the group to put ideas together and write a song. I wasn't sure this was possible, but we persevered. One girl started by singing "Praise the Lord" to chords I played on the piano then different people contributed and eventually we had a good song. When Adrian heard it, he was agreeably surprised and suggested that if we changed some of the lyrics using words from one of the Psalms, we could enter it for the Bible Society's Good News Song Competition. We won fourth prize and went with other prizewinners to the Royal Albert Hall to hear our song performed by a choir and to be presented with our prize by Cliff Richard. We had to do so much practising, walking on and off the stage, that I got rather bored and began to wonder whether all this preparation was really necessary. But when I actually went on the stage to meet Cliff it was worth it all. His warm personality came over immediately and I was most impressed. I had my photograph taken with him and it stands proudly on my mantlepiece at home.

# Twelve

# A Film Star

Sometimes when David Payne travelled abroad for Marshall Morgan and Scott, he played my tapes to business contacts. As a result I was invited to go to Norway in 1980, which was a great surprise to me. I needed a travelling companion and as it was in the school holidays, which of course suited me, Hilary was able to come. She had encouraged her brother Martin to look after the children himself and since he was a teacher the holidays were a good time for her to leave them with him. Much as she loved the children, they were not her own and at times she needed a break. A free trip to Norway was an excellent opportunity.

Not having done a concert tour before, I wasn't sure what to expect. We knew that we would be met at Oslo airport and booked into hotels in Oslo and Stavengar, and we had been told that all touring arrangements would be taken care of, but that was all. The advance publicity described me as a well-known Christian gospel artist and when one of the organisers said, "We hear that in England you are one of the best selling gospel singers," I wasn't too sure what to say. "I like doing this kind of thing," I replied casually. If they had realised this was my first concert tour, they might have been worried!

Hilary and I were taken to a plush hotel, put in a spacious double room and told that we would be contacted about being taken to concerts. The first evening we weren't sure whether we were expected to pay for our meals or not, so we chose the cheapest dishes on the hotel menu, but even they seemed expensive to us. Fortunately, we soon found out that the organisers were paying for our food as well. I found Norwegian food strange to start with, but enjoyed their hot chocolate drink topped with whipped cream.

Sometimes I sang in halls to eight hundred or even a thousand people. This was a terrific change as my largest audience until then had been about two hundred, but it was exhilarating. The sound engineers asked me what microphone I used and how much 'reverb' I liked, but I hadn't a clue! The Road Manager taught me some Norwegian phrases which I taped, and I practised saying them while travelling to concerts. Coming out with these gave me a good rapport with the audience and now whenever I appear abroad, I try to learn a few phrases in the language.

One night after I had been singing the audience began to clap their hands in a slow, rhythmic pattern. I went off stage feeling discouraged, thinking this meant they didn't like me. It actually meant that they wanted an encore and, much to my surprise, I was hustled back on stage.

Hilary and I found the Norwegian people shy at first but once we got to know them they were warm and friendly. Everyone went to a great deal of trouble preparing and presenting the food for us. There were always candles on the table and grace was said both at the beginning and at the end of every meal. I enjoyed the Norwegian hospitality, although eating in company can be embarrassing for a blind person. I was taught at school how to cut up food and eat 'politely', but it isn't always easy. When I'm eating out I have to ask someone to cut food up for me, especially steak, or to take meat off the bone. Otherwise I might end up with it on my knee!

At the end of the tour, one of the Norwegian organisers invited us to his home and we spent a very enjoyable evening with him. We had sold a lot of records and he was very surprised when I told them I had not done many concerts before. I am sure he was glad he hadn't known earlier! Hilary and I returned home after ten days and it was the first of many wonderful trips to Norway and other Scandinavian countries. Before our second visit, Hilary and I prayed specifically that we would get to know some Norwegians and as a result we became friendly with Astrid. She was sent to pick us up for a concert and when she realised we weren't occupied in the daytime offered to take us shopping. Our friendship developed and she has since been to stay with me in Watford. She has also sung with me at concerts and we have had a lot of fun together.

While on tour in one of the Scandinavian countries, Hilary and I were invited for a buffet lunch. Our hosts were delighted to have me in their home and kept plying me with food. I was the centre of the conversation and it made me feel as if I was really famous. Hilary was quiet as usual but when we left she was even quieter.

"Is there anything wrong?" I asked.

"No, not really," she replied.

"Are you sure?" I asked again.

"Well I suppose there is. I don't want you to be upset, but maybe you should know."

"Know what?"

"I wasn't given anything to eat - just one sandwich the whole time."

"What!" I was astonished.

"I know you didn't realise it, but they were so involved in talking to you that I was completely ignored. I'm not telling you this because I'm upset, but I think you should be aware that this kind of thing can happen."

I could hardly believe what she was saying and it came like a smack in the face. Basking in everyone's attention, and the false glory attached to it, I hadn't even tried to draw Hilary into the conversation.

This incident taught me a lesson. Hilary was so humble and unobtrusive, yet I couldn't have managed without her help. I'm part of a team ministry now and although I may be the figurehead, we all need each other if we're to do the job God has given us.

Marjorie, who had shared the house with me for two years, went off to Bible College that autumn. I was faced with the problem of looking for someone else to come and live with me and I didn't relish starting again. Living alongside another person means that we adjust to each other's way of life and become fond of one another, so to say goodbye is a wrench. The people who share my home are much more than lodgers.

Around this time a girl in her teens called Penny Misselbrook was eager to learn some of the chords of my songs. I tried to put her off because I was rather busy but she seemed determined, so eventually she came to my house and we had a very happy evening together. I then invited her to my birthday party and afterwards Marjorie said, "You know Marilyn, I can imagine young Penny living with you". I was surprised and replied, "But goodness she's only seventeen - there's too big an age gap."

Penny invited me to sing at her church and we got on incredibly well. One day she asked if I knew who was going to come into the house. "Not yet," I said, "but I have been praying that the Lord will show me." A week later Penny came up to me and said, "I know this sounds crazy but I think I may be the person to come and live with you".

I wasn't sure what to think, so I went to meet Penny's parents, who were lovely friendly people. They seemed in favour of the idea and I was beginning to feel it must be right, so we arranged for Penny to move in with me in October. Marjorie stayed for a few days to help Penny settle in. The first morning I wanted to show Penny my domestic capabilities so I went downstairs to make drinks. Whether it was because I wasn't awake I'm not sure, but I made one cup with only milk and water, one cup with tea and coffee mixed, and one black cup of coffee, instead of the planned two cups of coffee and one tea. What a laugh we had! To me there is nothing nicer than an early morning cup of tea and I kept up the ritual of bringing Penny a drink in bed. It was only three months later that she told me she didn't particularly like it!

Penny was a lively companion and very resourceful. At the time she moved in, *He Gives Joy* was becoming better known and there was an increase in the number of church meetings I was asked to take. Penny had a little Ford Escort and although she had only just passed her test, she was willing to travel all over the place to help me with my singing ministry. She would have liked to get involved in the Youth Group activities but she decided that God had sent her to live with me so that she could help me get to week-end concerts. So that is what she did, for which I will always be very grateful.

It was a hectic life for both of us - during the week I was teaching and Penny worked at the British Standards Institute in Hemel Hempstead. Often we would finish work on Friday and be away doing concerts all weekend, sometimes not returning home until the early hours of Monday morning. Penny looked after the house and garden as well so it was a completely new experience for her. I find certain aspects of housework frustrating because I can spend a long time hoovering, thinking that I have covered all of the room, only to be told by a sighted person that I have missed a bit in the middle or in the corner. Similarly with dusting, I don't get the satisfaction of seeing a shiny finished surface - the only way of knowing whether it is clean is by touch, which can mean fingerprints being left behind.

Penny's parents lived on a nearby farm and gave us eggs, corn on the cob and fresh vegetables when we visited. We often went to have Sunday tea with their large family of eight and it was interesting for me to see how they all related to each other - so different from being an only child.

After being with me for about six months, Penny began to feel very tired. Eventually the doctor told her to take time off work because she was suffering from nervous exhaustion. I felt guilty that she was doing so much for me - maybe we had made a mistake in deciding that she should come to live in the house. Some people suggested this to us and her parents were obviously concerned. Fortunately Penny recovered and bounced back to full health, so we assumed it was just the change in her routine which had caused her illness.

Now that I was doing more concerts, Mum decided that I should understand more about the use of cosmetics, so she took me to a department store in Birmingham. The beauty consultant showed me how to apply make-up myself but even with practice I don't find it easy to put it on evenly. Although I can manage if I have to, I prefer a friend to help so that I can feel more confident in the way I look.

Choosing the right style and colour of clothes, though enjoyable, is not always easy. I have to depend largely on the opinions of those who shop with me and I try to choose people who I have been told have got good taste. Bet even that can be confusing as tastes vary so much, so I go by the opinion of the majority! Sometimes I wish I knew more about colour instead of depending so much on someone else's choice. When an outfit feels comfortable I enjoy wearing it, and that is the main thing as far as I am concerned.

When I was in Canada I bought some metal braille tabs which can be stitched inside clothes to identify their colours. There are also colour coded buttons which can be obtained from the RNIB and enable me to know what colours I'm wearing.

It is difficult to know which colours match up, because as I do not remember seeing I have no concept of what colour is like. To me colours are just words with certain associations: people speak of a grey day, a red hot poker or a pitch black night.

Recently, Shirley Harbour became a *Colour Your World* consultant and analysed me for which colours suit me best. This has made a great deal of difference and as far as possible I try to stick to these colours. I know my clothes are more co-ordinated now.

About a year after Penny moved in Pam Chance who worked for CTVC - a Christian television company - rang me to say that she wanted to talk to me about making a film. I honestly thought this was a joke, but when she asked if she could come and meet me I realised that maybe it wasn't! When she arrived she explained that the company were doing a series called *Celebration* which was about people who had different talents and believed that God inspired them. By this time I had made another record called *Whispers of God* which was selling well. I didn't find making this second album such an ordeal because I now knew more about what was involved. Having heard it, Pam wanted to do a documentary about my life as a blind person, showing how my faith affected everyday living. It was to be called *Marilyn Baker Songwriter*. I was still amazed that this was happening to me and when I told my parents they were very excited and happily agreed to be interviewed.

For several months the camera almost ruled our lives - the film crew were around the house filming me feeding Yuma, cooking with Penny, giving music lessons, and generally doing the routine things of life. One scene shot at Chorleywood College showed me playing the oboe and Jean Coates accompanying me as we used to do.

A two hour concert was arranged with an invited audience at the television centre in Bushey so that flashbacks from it could be put into the twenty-eight minute documentary. Carol came to sing with me and it was really super to be together again. I wore an Indian style dress and performed with a group of instrumentalists brought together for the occasion. It was a great experience to be involved in a television production. The company were very good to us and treated us like stars. One scene showed Penny and me driving home after a late concert, and from then on the Ford Escort was nicknamed 'the film star banger'.

The congregation at St. James Road Baptist church were included in the film and Richard Harbour was interviewed. I was very touched by some of the things which were said by other friends. When Penny was asked, "Now what is she like to live with?" I wondered what she was going to say.

"She's quite a hilarious person really," Penny replied.

Carol told them I had an artistic temperament. I wasn't sure how to take that! Sue McClellan was asked to come to the studio to show how we recorded *He Gives Joy*, and it was lovely for the three of us to be together again.

When the film was finished it was shown on various independent television channels and sometimes repeated because of the demand. The biggest thrill though was when it won a bronze medal at the New York Film Festival. Some of the studio concert was put onto a separate film called *Marilyn Baker in Concert* and was also shown on some channels.

I had prayed before starting filming that I would really make the most of the experience and come over naturally. I knew it would be a tremendous opportunity to communicate God's love to people, and I think it did.

After feeling like a film star for a while and enjoying the 'high life' I came down to earth with a bump when I received the electricity bill for the quarter - the strong lights and equipment must have eaten up the units - but it had been a worthwhile experience and a tremendous privilege to be involved in making such a film.

Not long afterwards I went to Glasgow to appear in a Luis Palau Crusade where I met a lady called Willie

Jonker who works for a Dutch Christian broadcasting company. Willie asked me if I would go to Holland and appear on a TV programme which featured handicapped people whose faith had been a help to them.

At that time none of my friends were available to come with me but I agreed to go. Willie was going to book me into a hotel, but I didn't think that practical so she said I could stay with her. The night before going I panicked - I was going to travel to a foreign country, I didn't understand Dutch, I didn't know Willie very well and I had hardly done any filming. I thought how rash I had been to say I would go.

Willie met me at the airport and we travelled to Holland together. Because she wasn't used to having a blind person in her home, initially we both found it a little nerve-racking, but once I explained how she could help me best, we managed very well. At first when we walked anywhere, she was inclined to push me in front of her. This makes blind people feel insecure, so I showed her that if I hooked my arm into hers and let her go ahead she could lead me more easily. She loaned me some of her clothes when she realised that I didn't have much of a selection and explained that looking good on television was very important. The film had to compete with other secular productions so the standard had to be high, and I just wasn't used to this kind of professionalism in presentation.

In the studio I met a lovely Christian lady called Renata, who was also appearing on the programme. She had suffered from rheumatoid arthritis since a child and was in constant pain, but she didn't complain. I was most impressed by her manner.

I felt very much like a fish out of water, not being used to having such thick make-up plastered on or being prepared for filming so thoroughly. Willie went through the set questions with me and I practised the replies, but when it came to the recording session I found that the interviewer's English was not good and my answers did not flow well. In the end I just told my story to the people in the studio. It came across with much more feeling because I knew they were really interested.

Afterwards we returned to Willie's home and I was exhausted. The unfamiliarity of everything had left me feeling nervous and tense, and I decided that I would never again travel without an English-speaking companion, especially for such a major event as a film. It's not that it is impossible for me to travel on my own, but having someone to help me practically leaves me with energy to spare for more important things.

On the return flight from Holland I travelled as a first class passenger and the airline took great care of me, but I did have some difficulty in eating my meal. Airline trays are so tiny and I cut into my cake thinking it was a savoury. In the end I picked the food up with my fingers - it wasn't elegant, but I enjoyed it!

Willie and I became great friends and I returned to Holland many times, usually staying with her. Emilie, who shares the house with Willie, will often borrow a tandem from a neighbour so that I can ride on the back while she rides on the front. The cycle lanes in Holland make it quite safe and it's great fun.

As a result of these trips and appearances on television I have become quite well-known in Holland and have even been stopped in the streets by people who recognise me. Five minutes on television reaches more people than years of touring round a country.

# Thirteen

# On the Road

In the early spring of 1982 David Payne and his friend John Pac, who had produced *Whispers of God*, came to see me. They had been a real source of encouragement to me all through the period of my musical development and I had grown to respect and trust them. It came as a complete surprise when they said, "Marilyn, we want you to start considering something very important. We think that perhaps you ought to give up teaching and become a full time singer songwriter."

I was stunned! By this time I was teaching at five different schools and was happy in my work. I was doing quite well and had built up a good reputation. It hadn't occurred to me that God might ask me to give up my job. "I'll pray about it," I told David and John, but in my heart I had already decided: I wouldn't be prepared to finish teaching.

I didn't think that I would have the courage to let go of my security, but once I was on my own I remembered the words in Jeremiah Chapter 29 verse 11: "'For I know the plans I have for you,' declares the Lord, 'plans to prosper you and not to harm you, plans to give you hope and a future.'" I believed that God did know what His plans were so I prayed:

"Lord show me in a way that I can understand what You want for my future. I know that what I think is right isn't necessarily the way You want me to go. Please make clear what Your plan is."

It had taken me a long time to build up my teaching practice and I knew that if I gave up the work in schools, it would be very difficult to get back into it again. If I was to take this step, I had to be sure it was part of God's plan for me. Over a period of three weeks it became increasingly clear that it was. The Sunday after my visit from David and John, a man came to speak at my church. He explained that he had been teaching in a public school, where he had been in a senior post, when he felt God calling him out of teaching and into pastoral work. Eventually he did give up his job but it was a hard struggle: he loved his profession, felt secure in his work and was in line for further promotion. I thought how similar our positions were.

A few days later I was singing at a church when the preacher said how easy it is to find excuses for not doing what the Lord has told us. I felt he was speaking to me - especially when he read Hebrews Chapter 12 verse 25: "See to it that you do not refuse him who speaks"!

When I spoke to Mum and Dad about the possibility of becoming a full time singer, initially they did not think it a good idea, and warned me that it would be difficult to return to teaching once I had given it up. But when I spoke to them later, I was surprised to discover that they felt, on reflection, that perhaps I should take the opportunity if it meant more openings for me, especially if it meant I could travel. But the decision was up to me: nobody else could make it for me.

There remained only one obstacle. One of my private pupils was a very gifted oboist and I knew she wanted to be a professional musician. I had been involved with her and her parents for several years and wanted to remain so, but the Lord took away the last thing I was holding onto: my pupil told me that she had decided to give up oboe lessons while she was taking her 'O' levels because she felt that she couldn't cope with all the work.

I knew than what I had to do. I gave in my notice at the different schools to finish at the end of the summer term in 1982.

When I reflected on my decision I said to myself, "What on earth have you done? Where's the work going to come from?" But two days later, much to my amazement I was offered a two month tour of Australia and New Zealand, starting in October. It was such a surprise because I hadn't realised that anyone there had even heard of me. I was delighted to accept and could hardly believe I was going to the other side of the world. The timing of the invitation was perfect and it came as confirmation that I had done the right thing in giving up teaching.

There was however one problem. With this new way of life, it was no longer going to be possible to have Yuma as my guide dog. There would be no routine for her to follow and I knew she wouldn't be happy travelling so much of the time. Reluctantly, I had to accept that we would have to be parted.

I had come to depend on Yuma - she knew the routes to the local shops and other places I visited regularly. Without her I would have to start using a long cane. Even ten minutes with the cane left me tired. It meant concentrating, not only on finding the way but also on avoiding obstacles. With a guide dog the same walk could be relaxing and enjoyable.

Because her working life was almost over anyway, it was agreed that Yuma could go to live with my parents. It was a good arrangement because I knew she would be well looked after - and probably spoilt - by Mum and Dad, and I would be able to see her when I visited them. Yuma settled down well and really loved her new lifestyle.

As well as losing Yuma, this new way of life posed me with other problems. How could I possibly manage travelling, getting myself organised, staying in other people's homes and learning my way around new places? I needed a sighted person to travel with me. People who can see can quickly look round a room and understand the layout. In a strange bathroom or bedroom they can immediately see where everything is and decide where to put their belongings, but a blind person needs time to work out the appropriate place to put things. If we lose something it can take a while to relocate it, whereas a sighted person would spot it immediately.

I've certainly had some embarrassing moments. On one occasion I was staying in a couple's home and proceeded to undress in what I thought was my bedroom. What I didn't realise was that I had turned the wrong way when I came out of the bathroom and I was in fact in my host's and hostess's room The husband was cleaning his teeth at the wash basin with his back to me. I had assumed it was the friend I was sharing a room with, so imagine my consternation when the wife walked in exclaiming, "Oh my dear, you're in the wrong room!" It was a terrible mistake, but fortunately the couple took it in good part.

Such experiences highlighted my need of a sighted companion. I needed someone who, as well as taking care of practical details, would be able to pray with me and share the planning of programmes for my concerts. When two close friends felt that God might want them to travel with me, I had a difficult choice to make. After much prayer and discussion it was decided that Penny Misselbrook should be the one. She had completed a year's course at London Bible College that summer and did not have another job to go to. As well as talking to organisers and arranging the sale of records after concerts, she would be able to help with singing and playing the guitar.

The first major event Penny and I took part in was the Christian Holiday Convention at Filey in September. It was a really good week for us both, but it suddenly hit me how much I missed teaching. It seemed strange not to have school bells governing my life and even stranger to be somewhere other than school in September!

Our trip to Australia and New Zealand drew near and

we needed lots of different vaccinations, partly because we were stopping off at Jakarta. I had just had an injection for cholera when I went to sing at a ladies' meeting. Just as I reached the climax and was saying, "Now God has a plan for your life ..." the piano stool collapsed underneath me. I was sprawled on the floor surrounded by hymn books and bits of paper. When some alarmed ladies rushed to help me all I could think of was the pain after my vaccination and I shouted loudly, "Get off my arm". After that disturbance it was difficult to finish the meeting with dignity! For a long time after that episode I was reluctant to trust any piano stool. By the time I was invited back to this church a couple of years later, however, I was sure they would have replaced theirs. When the minister told me they had only mended it, I asked for a chair instead!

When the day of our flight finally came I could hardly contain my excitement about going 'down under'. We travelled by Geruda Airlines and had some difficulty trying to communicate with the Indonesian crew in English, although they were very charming. We did enjoy the food, although 'rice cooked in banana leaves' and 'chicken with hot chilli peanut sauce' didn't turn out to be quite what I had expected.

Due to a mix-up about travelling dates we were booked to do a concert on the evening of our arrival. This was at the home of Pearl and Peter Sumner where we were staying. Pearl and Peter are directors of an organisation in Australia which puts Christian literature into braille and onto cassettes for blind people. I really don't know how we got through the concert and I can clearly remember the floor rocking! But we managed and I was enthusiastically looking forward to experiencing the Australian way of life. We then travelled from Sydney to Melbourne on to Brisbane to sing at an evening event arranged by *Youth for Christ*. It was so hot that we had to have the air conditioning on overnight in the hotel room. The next morning we got up early to wander to the shops where we bought fresh pineapple and tropical fruits. It was in Brisbane that we went to a Wildlife Park and I had my photograph taken cuddling a koala bear. His fur felt soft as he snuggled into me and I was surprised at how heavy he was and how sharp his claws were.

I really enjoyed the casual way of life of the Australians and it was a great experience to meet so many super people. We continued our tour by going on to the North and South Islands of New Zealand. Although there weren't vast crowds attending the concerts, those who did come bought a great number of records, which meant that in the end the tour did finance itself.

Owing to a misunderstanding Penny and I didn't have much spending money. This was disappointing because we had hoped to buy Christmas presents, but an English couple we stayed with unexpectedly presented us each with a cheque, saying that God had told them to give us this money. We were of course delighted and very thankful to them and to the Lord for His provision - and proceeded to buy some very unusual gifts for family and friends. This experience showed me how much God cared by providing for us financially just when we needed it.

One particular church near Auckland amazed me. Its design was based on an American idea. The pulpit area could be dropped to the level of an orchestra pit or raised to the same height as the congregation. About twelve hundred people attended this church and the crêche facilities were fantastic. There were over a hundred small beds so that young children could sleep while their parents were attending meetings. Babies could stay in the car because frequent patrols went round the car park and parents could be contacted by radio if necessary. It really was most unusual.

The thing which impressed me most about New Zealand churches though was the sense of worship, love and openness which I found in many of them. Often the atmosphere was prepared by a period of worship and deep ministry before I sang and spoke and I don't know who was blessed most. There was such a refreshing joy and freedom and many people's lives were touched.

When I knew we were going to Rotarua I wanted to go into one of the famous sulphur springs. But the pools closed early and our concerts ended late. Much to Penny's embarrassment I announced one evening, towards the end of the meeting, "Now we've got to hurry along so that I can get to one of the hot pools".

Many people apologised for holding me up and I began to feel rather guilty but the problem was solved when we met a hotel owner who offered us the use of his hotel's private pool. The smell of sulphur was like rotten eggs but I soon forgot that in the luxury of lying back in the hot water and relaxing after a hectic day!

The tour organisers had made a card available so that people could say what they thought of the concert. Most of the comments were complimentary but I was shocked to learn that one said, "Deadly boring. A wasted opportunity for Jesus Christ. She sings about Jesus changing us, so let's hope that He begins to do something in her life." I couldn't put these remarks to the back of my mind and said to Alistair, the road manager, "Do you think there is any truth in it? Maybe it's just an old-fashioned person who doesn't like my style of music." After a while I asked Alistair if the card had been signed.

I roared with laughter when he told me the name was Luigi Macaroni, and Alistair wondered what was going on. Luigi Macaroni was a comic opera character I had made up, and I realised that Penny must have written the card. The joke had gone down just as she had hoped!

Towards the end of the tour my spiritual batteries were running low and I felt tired. It was quite a strain to sing nearly every night, telling people something meaningful and fresh each time, but it had been a wonderful trip and I wouldn't have missed the experience for anything. We ended our stay by having a few days break in Jalon and as we walked in the bush and enjoyed the sunshine we found it hard to believe that in a few days time we would be back home in England spending a traditional Christmas.

# Fourteen

# Rest in My Love

David Payne agreed to become my manager around this time and his wife Marilyn organised the bookings - all free of charge. They helped Penny and me in many ways and their friendship still means a great deal.

In the new year we toured with *Prepare the Way*, a nationwide presentation to prepare people for Mission England. It seemed strange to be working alongside people I had always held in high esteem in the Christian world. The whole idea of being a full-time Christian singer, and much more in the public eye, was still new to me, and sometimes I found the responsibility a little frightening. I couldn't get used to the fact that people really took notice of things I said and that they commented, sometimes months later, on what I had sung or spoken about during concerts.

I missed having contact with my friends at Chorleywood College, particularly Jean and Beryl. It wasn't as easy to get back there now that I was 'on the road' but I tried to return for the annual Old Girls' Reunion as often as I could until the school's closure in 1987.

Mum and Dad took a great deal of interest in where I went and what I did. I visited them as much as possible and in May 1983 I had a strange experience while I was standing in the kitchen with Mum. She was telling me how a few days earlier she had choked on a piece of bacon.

"You know love," she said "that really frightened me. For a moment I thought I was going to die."

At that moment a voice said to me quite clearly, "Tell

her about My love. Tell her the Gospel message." There was an urgency within me and I knew I had to talk to her straightaway.

"You don't have to be afraid of death Mum," I said gently. "God really cares about you and He wants you to belong to Him. All you've got to do is accept the fact that God loved you so much that He sent his Son to take the blame on His shoulders for all the wrong things you've ever done. If you do that it means that when you meet God face to face you won't meet him as your judge but as your father."

Although Mum listened she made no comment and I wondered why I had been so compelled to talk to her in this way. I pushed the incident to the back of my mind, but I was forced to recall it only two months later when I was recording the album *Refresh me Lord* at ICC Studios in Eastbourne that July. While we were in the middle of the recording Dad phoned me to say that Mum was far from well and was to go into hospital. He asked if I could collect Yuma because he felt he couldn't cope with taking care of her, giving her the exercise and attention she needed, as well as looking after the home and visiting Mum.

It all came as a great shock to me and I sensed there was something seriously wrong. Mum and I had always been very close and I knew that she had aged in the last six months. She had always had a lot of energy and was the fittest in the family, but when we had gone for walks with Yuma recently, I had noticed that she got tired and breathless easily, that her walk was slower and that even her voice was shaky at times.

Dad was in the process of giving up his garage and he and Mum had been talking about touring the country in a caravanette and spending more time in their Welsh holiday home, so this came as a sudden blow to them.

Penny drove all the way from Eastbourne to pick up Yuma from Birmingham. Yuma was bewildered by the change in her surroundings and found it difficult to adjust to being in a recording studio instead of enjoying the luxuries of retirement, but it was nice for me to see her again.

One of the songs on the album was *Rest in My Love, Relax in My Care* and the words imagine God speaking to us personally, telling us not to be anxious or worried. They came to me one day during an anxious bus journey to visit Hilary who lived in Aylesbury. I had several connections to make and I wasn't even sure if I had ended up on the right bus or what time Hilary would be meeting me at the other end. I felt quite panicky, but once I had established that I *was* on the right bus, I relaxed and talked to the Lord about it. I felt Him reply, "If you'd only rested in My love and remembered that I was taking care of you, you wouldn't have got into such a flap."

Singing the song now for the record was exceptionally poignant, because more than ever I needed to 'rest in His love and relax in His care'. Tears were in my eyes as I thought of Mum - I so much wanted to be with her but I knew I wouldn't be able to do anything to help. John Pac was particularly kind and considerate and after we had recorded the song we prayed that God would give me the peace and courage I needed. We also asked that He would hold Mum 'safe in His care' as the song said.

After recording *Refresh me Lord* I was booked to sing at *Royal Week*, a family holiday conference in Cornwall. I rang Dad most nights and it was very hard being so far away and not able to see Mum. Although I had sensed that she was seriously ill it was still a staggering blow when I heard that she had leukaemia. I wept bitterly after I heard the news and a doctor on the team tried to console me, saying that leukaemia is often treatable. Several people from my church were also at *Royal Week* and were very supportive but inside I felt devastated. I cried because I didn't know how to cope with Mum's illness. Although people tried to help, they couldn't get inside me and really understand my inner anguish. Feeling as I did, it was very difficult to sing some of my songs.

Over the next few weeks and months Mum went in and out of hospital several times to have chemotherapy. I was amazed to see how bravely she faced up to the treatment. She felt very sick, but I was grateful that she didn't suffer from depression. I visited her in hospital as much as possible, and as she had a room on her own she welcomed the company. I would sit close to her bed as we talked about what I was doing and where I had been. Because Mum had always been so fit, Dad had relied on her to look after the domestic side of their life, so it was particularly hard for him now that he had to keep things going at home. He also found it strange not going to work at the garage. Dad and I found it difficult to communicate our fears to each other and it really was a traumatic time for both of us.

Mum was in hospital for Christmas of that year. At home Dad and I tried to be festive, but it just didn't work. Dad cooked a turkey leg and I helped as best I could but it is difficult for me to work in someone else's kitchen where items aren't labelled and I don't know where things are kept.

Dudley Road Hospital tried to give the patients a good time at Christmas and Mum's only concern was how we were coping. We spent the afternoon together, but it seemed so sad to be spending Christmas with her in hospital. She came home a few days later but she was so frail that I was worried that she would fall over and hurt herself as she already had on several occasions. She was also very vulnerable to picking up infections so we were constantly 'guarding' her one way or another.

Before returning to Watford I spent a few days with a close friend Cathy Ruskin and her parents in Wales. Cathy and I had been good friends for several years. We always enjoyed each other's company and often had outings together. While we were in Wales she took me to a local sports centre where we relaxed in a jacuzzi and I enjoyed my first experience of a sauna. We went tobogganing on the mountains and she suggested we record some of the things we had done so that we could send a tape to Mum.

In spite of my holiday I returned to Watford feeling tense and ill. I couldn't sleep and I felt as if my whole inside was shaking. Why wasn't I coping better emotionally? As a Christian I thought that I should be strong, but I wasn't and I felt guilty.

To make matters worse I was also trying to get used to a new companion-helper on the road. During 1983 Penny had become unwell and had come to the reluctant decision that at the end of the year she would have to stop travelling with me. It was a real blow because she was so easy to get on with, so adaptable and sociable, that I couldn't imagine anyone being able to take her place. We had worked so well together that I dreaded having to find a replacement, but at least she would still be living with me, which was some consolation.

I made the need of a new helper known through my prayer letter and met Morfudd Bowen through her sister who lived locally. Although she had a Welsh name Morfudd had lived in Cheshire for most of her life. She was well-qualified for her new role. Like Penny she was a good organiser and extremely practical, and also very musical.

Morfudd was given accommodation in one of the church houses. Although I was feeling far from well I didn't want her to know so I tried to put on a brave face, but that probably made it harder for her. I felt I had to be strong, not wanting to load Morfudd with my sadness.

Because I woke each morning about 2.30 and couldn't get off to sleep again I became very tired and found it more and more difficult to relax. I kept trying to appear as if I was coping, but it was obvious to me that I wasn't. After a bit of persuasion I went to my G.P. who prescribed some mild tranquillizers, which actually didn't work. They made me go from one extreme to another, wanting either to laugh or to cry all the time.

During the first week that Morfudd joined me she drove me to East London to sing at a mother and baby hospital. She had not long passed her driving test and had never driven in London so she was very nervous about the whole affair, especially as she also had to navigate. It was pouring with rain and we had a slight bump. This upset Morfudd but all I could do was laugh, which wasn't very helpful! We eventually arrived at our destination feeling fraught, but managed to do the concert. Pat Wright, one of the helpers, led us to the motorway afterwards and we were very grateful. It was months before Morfudd got used to driving in London.

# Fifteen

# New Continents

In February Mum began to get a little better. She started to gain weight and the chemotherapy seemed to be helping. She was able to be at home for longer periods and life seemed to settle down a bit for us all.

I was discovering what a joy it was to work with someone as musical as Morfudd. She was a good singer and played both the guitar and piano. In concerts, she would harmonize with me and even sing solos occasionally. Because our voices were both low, Morfudd had to practise hitting the high notes in order to sing above me, but the end result was very pleasing.

In June, we were due to go on a tour in South Africa. Now that Mum's health had picked up, I felt much better in myself and I was eagerly looking forward to travelling to another continent.

I wanted to find out as much as I could about black people in South Africa, particularly how Christian black people felt about Christian whites and vice versa. One thing which I was pleased to notice when I arrived was that many white Christians treated black people with respect and did feel the injustice being done to them. I was surprised at the differences in values and outlook between black and white people. For instance I noticed that the servants who called all of us white people 'Madam' had a great pride in their job. One day when Morfudd went to wash up the maid was very indignant. She exclaimed that that was her job and banned Morfudd from the kitchen! One lady told me that a black maid who worked for her had a daughter who had been offered a place in university. The daughter had become pregnant and decided not to take the place so my friend said to her mother, "Isn't that sad. You must feel disappointed." The black maid replied, "I feel that you don't understand us Madam. The most important thing as far as I'm concerned is to know that my daughter is healthy and can bear children."

I felt a tremendous expectancy about what God could and would do among His people there, but there were certain aspects in some churches which bothered me. We met some Christians whom I would call 'spiritual casualties' - people who felt that they had let God down because they hadn't been able to believe enough for healing and power in their lives. Great emphasis was being placed on the healing power of God and many people felt that it was their fault that they had not received healing. They were trying to live up to the expectations of their leaders and losing sight of the other things God wanted to do in their lives.

I am very thankful for that time in South Africa because I feel the Lord used me to show some of those people that God accepts them as they are, not because of what they achieve in their spiritual lives. It was lovely too to be with Christians so full of faith and love for God, and there was no doubt that the Lord was moving in a wonderful way among them.

We met some fantastic people that month and because we couldn't get a flight back at the end of it we stayed on an extra week and went to the Kruger National Park. Although I couldn't see the animals I could certainly hear them! I bought a cassette of the different sounds including lions, elephants and monkeys, which gave me an insight into their behaviour. We also had lots of barbeques, called 'brys'. These were great fun and I thoroughly enjoyed the outdoor way of life.

When we got home I only had a few days to spare before going to America. I wanted to spend time with

Mum and Dad so it was a marvellous surprise to find that Mum was well enough for them to travel from Birmingham to Watford to stay with me. We had a really good time together before I flew to New York with Carol Franklin. I had always longed to go to America - it was the dream of a lifetime - so I was extremely excited at the prospect. Now that Mum's health was reasonably stable, I felt happier about leaving her.

One reason for going was to attend the Christian Booksellers Convention being held at Anaheim, Los Angeles. David Payne had by this time started up his own record company called *Window* and I was one of the artists recording on that label. The sales team had gone to this conference and I went with a view to meeting a record producer who we hoped would bring out an album for me in the States.

From New York, Carol and I flew on to Los Angeles via St. Louis. For some reason we changed motels every night once we had arrived but at least during the day we had the wonderful facilities of the Anaheim Hilton, where David and the managing directors of other record companies were staying. Their sunbathing area intrigued me because it had artificial grass which didn't feel anything like real grass and in the flowerbeds little speakers in the shape of mushrooms gave out background music. It all seemed rather artificial.

We had the opportunity to go to Disneyland and as it was Donald Duck's fiftieth birthday everything was centred around him. I was fascinated by the whole place, even though originally I hadn't been particularly interested in going there. The thought of going on some of the big roller coasters turned my stomach and I felt much happier on the quieter rides. There was a tremendous atmosphere and we had great fun. It was an experience I'm glad I didn't miss.

One ambition of mine has always been to ride in a Rolls Royce and I was able to do this in Hollywood when we visited a millionaire. Unfortunately he had had a stroke and couldn't speak to us but we enjoyed our visit. My ride in the Rolls wasn't quite what I expected and I preferred the American Cadillac - to me it seemed more comfortable and quieter.

I met the singer Kelly Willard at our hotel. Kelly is a well-known Christian artist in the States and she took Carol and me to the Vineyard Fellowship, John Wimber's church, the following weekend. Even though vast numbers were present, it was a most relaxing and peaceful experience.

We then moved on to Nashville where I met Ray Nenow, who was going to produce my next record, and his wife Brenda. We were invited to a barbeque and even though I only drank a little wine I got the hiccups! They got worse when I giggled because I was embarrassed and I must have given a bad impression. Although Ray was amused I found out later that he did think I had drunk too much! The barbeque was great fun however and we had a good time that evening.

While in Nashville we visited Opres land and I bought a cowboy hat from one of the many souvenir shops. Nearly everyone we met in Nashville seemed to be making a record and expectations were high. It was a lazy but exciting city where everyone was friendly and the southern drawl sounded just like the voices I had heard on American films. Even after I returned home my head was still spinning with all that I had experienced.

# Sixteen

# Management Group

Not long after I got back to England, Mum's health began to deteriorate. A chest infection made her particularly ill. Dad phoned asking me to go to Birmingham as it wasn't likely that she would pull through this time. When I received a phone call like this I always went to pieces inside. Fortunately Morfudd was marvellous and, as on previous occasions, took control, packed my case, sorted out details and drove me to Birmingham.

After visiting Mum in hospital I became increasingly concerned that she would turn to God and be able to face death knowing that she was loved by Him. I agonised in my mind as to how to pray. I wanted to pray for healing but deep within me I knew that I didn't have the faith to believe that a miracle would happen.

I was booked to sing at a mission where Jean Darnall was speaking. Her talk was inspiring and at the end she prayed that God would give every person in the room saving faith. When I returned home I thought about how to pray for Mum again and God said, "Pray that your mother will be given saving faith". Faith is a gift and so many people who cannot believe have got barriers in their hearts which need breaking down. So that is what I prayed that evening, simply but earnestly. A couple of days later when I visited Mum in hospital I sat on the bed talking to her. We had a lovely time even though she was so ill. I talked to her about the things I was doing and told her about my concerts, as I wanted her to feel involved with my life. Then she said to me, "I can't imagine what it's going to be like when I go into that coffin. I can't think that this is just the end of my life."

"Death needn't be the end Mum. God loves you so much that He wants to give you the assurance that when you die you will be accepted by Him," I replied quietly.

"It's all very well for you, Marilyn, because you've lived your life as a Christian. You've included God, but I haven't."

"I know Mum, but it's not too late, you know."

Mum listened before adding, "I just wish I knew that God could accept me". She paused. "I'm going to pray."

"Do pray Mum, because He's here with us now," I said, hardly believing my ears.

She prayed a simple prayer: "Please God, I want to belong to You. Make me Your child and please look after me. Amen."

I knew that my mother had prayed to God in the past, especially when things had been difficult in her life. But this time it was different. She was handing her life over into His hands.

With tears in my eyes I said, "Mum, that means that you are totally forgiven now. When Jesus died on the cross, He took all the blame for everything you've ever done and all you have to do is believe that it's true."

"It seems almost too simple, doesn't it?" she asked. "Almost too simple to believe that He could accept us like that."

"We're going to be given new bodies Mum. One day we shall live again and there will be no more sickness or pain."

Even though my mother was drowsy with medication she commented wryly, "I hope we don't treat the new bodies the same way we treated the old ones".

From that day onwards, although Mum didn't talk much about what had happened, she had a peacefulness about her which was certainly not there before and she wanted people to pray with her. If the hospital chaplain came to visit her, she was always sad if he left without prayer. Her thoughts had been lifted to a new dimension.

Just before I returned to America in October for the recording of my record with Ray, Penny Misselbrook went to work with David Payne in Hampshire. She had lived with me for four years and we knew it was time for her to move on. I needed a friend to share expenses and jobs around the house and a sighted person seemed the obvious choice. I was surprised when after praying one morning I felt God saying to me very clearly that He wanted my blind friend Penny Cooze to come and join me. It wasn't an audible voice, but deep inside His voice penetrated into my being and I recognised it.

I rang Penny, who was temporarily living with her mother in Somerset, and asked her what she thought - she sounded stunned at first and then explained that she had been praying for quite a while that she would be able to move nearer London. Several people had suggested she ask me for accommodation, but seeing that I only had two bedrooms and Penny Misselbrook was living with me, she hadn't done so. Penny said she would think and pray about the idea and within a week she had decided that she would come to Watford, even though we were both uncertain as to how it would work out.

The timing wasn't good because Penny moved in with me five days before I was due to go to America to record the album in Nashville. She had not looked after a house on her own before and certainly didn't know the routes around to the shops, I was very apprehensive about leaving her alone. I talked about it to the Lord and He assured me that I should trust Him to look after Penny, who would be safe in His care.

Kelly Willard, (whom I had become friendly with while in America in the summer) was in Britain with her husband Dan and little boy Bryan. They visited me in Watford and we spent a happy day together just before I flew off to the States with Morfudd.

As we didn't do a lot of recording until late afternoon we had mornings free, but not having a car we were restricted in what we could to. As local phone calls in America are free, I phoned the tourist information centres for suggestions and was surprised at how helpful they were. Sometimes Morfudd and I travelled to various places on the bus. We enjoyed these outings very much and met some really interesting people. At other times we stayed in, sampling the many television channels and even becoming hooked on some soap operas! Morfudd would describe what was happening on the screen if the dialogue didn't make it clear.

The actual recording of the record went very well and the musicians, although expensive to hire, were superb. They listened to what I said, quickly grasped what I meant and wanted to build on my ideas. It was wonderful working with them.

Morfudd and I only stayed in the States for ten days so I wasn't really involved in the musical arrangements of the songs and left the producer to finish off the tracks and put the instrumentals and backing vocals together. The finished result didn't sound like any of my previous records and somehow we lost some of the intimacy which I like, but the quality was excellent and I had to remember that this album was made for the American market.

When I returned home I found that Penny had coped remarkably well. Everything was more organised than when I had left. She had put a braille plan on the freezer door, had labelled tins and put things in logical sequence. She seemed to have the household affairs running like clockwork!

Later that month Ian Valkeith joined our ministry to be our full-time sound engineer. There were now three of us instead of two to support and this meant a new step in trusting God for our needs, but David Payne had realised how important it was for us to have good amplification at our concerts.

Around this time some of the leaders and members of my church, St. James Road Baptist, felt it would be a good idea to form a management group consisting of representatives from our own and other churches. The role of the group still hasn't changed. It is to pray with the team, and to decide on business policies and the direction the ministry should take. David Payne was on the group and acted as consultant to us all, which was good because he was still very much involved in our work. We also became a registered charitable trust - Marilyn Baker Ministries - and some of the management group became trustees.

When Ian joined the team it was decided that we needed to purchase P.A. equipment, which was a big step as it was not only expensive but also changed our whole method of operating. We now needed to arrive at least an hour and a half before each concert started to set up our equipment.

Often we had found that halls or churches didn't have adequate microphones, which meant that I had to sing loudly. As soon as we had our amplification system working we found that I got fewer sore throats and we could feel confident of achieving a good sound quality no matter where we went.

It hadn't been a sudden decision to increase our team. We found that we were being invited to do more and more concerts and it wasn't possible for Morfudd to continue coping with the organisation, driving and navigating and playing in the concert, as well as helping me get ready. It was amazing how well she did all these things, seemingly at the same time!

I had met Ian three years earlier when I went to visit Penny Cooze. They both worked for Torch Trust and when she and Ian started going out together they sometimes rang to see if they could come to Watford because living in the community at Torch Trust as they did wasn't very conducive to having a romantic relationship. Ian had always shown a great deal of interest in my work and said that he would like to help on the technical side.

Penny and Ian's relationship didn't develop and Penny went to do a year's course at London Bible College. Ian still kept in contact with me and after a while we began to think that God might want him to come and work with us. It was a difficult decision because I wasn't sure how the relationship would work between Penny and Ian. But I needn't have worried - they got on well together and their relationship is like that of a close brother and sister now. In addition I wasn't sure where money would come from to support us all. On our literature we emphasised that we didn't demand a set fee but that we wanted churches or organisations to give what they could honestly afford. When Ian joined the team we didn't advertise that we needed more money, but found that the giving automatically increased. This was a real sign that God had His hand on our work and we were reminded of the truth 'My God will supply all your needs according to his riches in glory in Christ Jesus'.

The following May Ian got married to Ruth, a girl he had met whilst working at Torch Trust. She took over the administration for our bookings from Marilyn Payne, who found it too much to cope with now that she had started working.

# Seventeen

# An Uphill Struggle

We had a very heavy schedule with lots of travelling, and trying to cope with Mum's deteriorating illness took its toll. By Christmas 1984 I began to feel really ill. Dad and I had been told that the chemotherapy wasn't working and we knew it was now only a matter of time. Mum still needed to go into hospital regularly for blood transfusions and managed to be very brave. She could hardly walk and one day she rang me and cried in agony over the phone. It made me angry and I wanted to know where God was in all this suffering. I couldn't understand how He could allow this to happen. Why? It didn't make sense.

Our concert schedule started again in January but I began to find it more and more difficult to keep going. Getting up in the mornings was awful and I felt as if I was going to collapse. I felt really ill - it was much more than being upset. The shaking inside started again, and it was much worse than before. My hands became itchy and sensitive, which made touching or handling things difficult. My stomach became upset and I developed many extreme physical symptoms. It was thought I might have a viral infection, but nothing definite was found. Strangely, my friend Cathy also had the same symptoms.

For the first time I knew what real depression was. Even the smallest thing seemed impossible to cope with, and after talking it over with Penny, I realised that I couldn't carry on doing concerts so I rang David Payne and explained. He was very supportive, told me I needed a complete break and said that he would write to explain the situation to the concert organisers. A group called

*Lovelight* did one or two of my bookings for me very successfully.

The depression increased. I didn't want to face anyone or even to go outside. Eventually I started taking mild tranquillizers, but I wasn't happy about it. Penny was a terrific help. At times I felt I couldn't pray, but she prayed for me and with me. Penny believed that God wanted to dig deeper within me and heal me of some of the emotional scars and difficulties I had experienced over the years, in much the same way as He had dealt with her. She understood how much I was grieving about the suffering my mother was going through. The emotional strain of being told that Mum was going to die soon, then being told that she was improving slightly, had become almost unbearable.

God showed through prophecies to Penny and friends that it was a time when He was going to restore me physically but more than that, He would make me a much stronger person emotionally and spiritually. Because of all the difficulties Penny had faced and come through she was sensitive to my feelings and always willing to listen. Sometimes when I couldn't sleep, she sat listening or talking to me for hours.

It was hard trying to hide my depression from my parents but I'm sure that Mum knew and she often told me not to worry about her. Her health deteriorated quite rapidly during these weeks and eventually she was put on morphine, which we realised would make her unconscious most of the time. I visited her with Cathy on the first day she started the injections. The morphine deadened the pain so that she was more relaxed and happy than she had been for a long time. Cathy had not met my mother before so I was glad that she was able to see her like this. We all laughed and joked together and it was the last rational conversation which Mum and I had. Soon the heavy doses of morphine took their toll and she became incoherent, so visiting her was very hard. After she had been on morphine for eight days the hospital phoned to say that Dad and I had better go to see her because she was getting weaker and wasn't expected to live much longer. I wanted to go straightaway but Dad was undecided. He didn't know if he could face being with her when she died, but because I knew that she had committed herself to Jesus, I wanted to be there and help her. Even though I knew she couldn't speak I felt that she would hear me, but I understood how Dad felt so we waited until the usual visiting times.

We arrived at 2.45pm and I sat by the bed holding Mum's hand. Dad said sadly, "I think she's going to die. I think this is it". I could hardly believe it could happen so quickly in the end. He went to get the nurse and Mum breathed in a strangled sort of way. I knew Dad was right and said, "Mum you are going to be with the Lord Jesus now and this is not really goodbye because one day I'll be with you again". I knew she heard me. Then she stopped breathing.

The timing was amazing - the Lord knew how much I wanted to be with her at the end.

I was surprised at how peaceful I felt afterwards as we made our way home. The agony of going backwards and forwards to visit was over. I felt calm. During Mum's illness I had often wondered how I would feel when she finally died - whether I would be sure that she was with the Lord - but I knew for certain that she was. I *knew* she was alive: it was and is an inner conviction that nothing can shake. Although the suffering she went through has left its mark on me and will never be forgotten, the thing that comforts me more than anything is to know that God has wiped away her tears for ever and that she is in His presence. I feel a real loss yet I have experienced the comfort of my Heavenly Father.

The funeral service was not a very good one - the vicar seemed uninterested - but in the end I decided that didn't really matter. I knew where Mum was and that was the important thing.

Very gradually I began to feel better physically and spiritually. I often thought of the story of a man who talked to God as he looked back over his life:

"Why is it that in parts of my life I can see two sets of footprints in the sand and I know that You are walking beside me? But in some of the most difficult times it looks as if You have left me because there is only one set of prints."

"No I never left you," God replied. During these difficult times I was carrying you."

That was what God did for me. It was when I realised that He wasn't expecting me to be on top of things, and that He wanted to carry me and help me through, that I began to experience the healing and love I needed. He didn't condemn my grief in any way because it was a natural reaction. He showed me that He understood how I felt and shared my sorrow. The Bible says that, 'In all our distress He was distressed' and I knew He was.

At the end of March I resumed work. I still got tired easily and didn't have a lot of stamina but I managed, though my sleeping pattern was upset for quite a long time.

In the summer Carol Franklin and I went to Canada again for a month to visit her Auntie Joan and Uncle Nick. We had a relaxing time and it was just what I needed. One particular raft trip down some rapids was a memorable experience. I laughed and screamed all the way down and the guide, realising how much I was enjoying myself, tried to get me as wet as possible. It was a marvellous sensation. We were in Alberta at the time of the famous Calgary Stampede, and although we didn't go to the stadium we could feel its atmosphere, which was like that of a wild west town.

We had some super barbeques and I really enjoyed the outdoor life, but when I got home it was impossible to get into some of the clothes that had previously fitted me - the food had been too wonderful!

Before going to Canada I had developed back trouble due to a trapped sciatic nerve and this caused me a lot of pain on holiday. I had some chiropractic treatment but it didn't help much. Once back home I sought medical help and had physiotherapy and traction treatment but both were unsuccessful. Travelling to concerts became a problem but was compensated for by the fact that many people seemed to be responding to God's challenge on their lives at this time.

# Eighteen

# A New Thing

Dad found it hard to cope with life without Mum. She had always been the hub of the family, but domestically he has learnt to cope well. Now when I go to see him, he cooks simple but lovely meals for us and we have some happy times together. I cannot be the companion to him that Mum was and he cannot be the special friend she was to me. Our relationship to each other is different from what we had with Mum and we both have to accept that life without her can never be the same. But I realise that Dad's loneliness is far greater than mine, because I have the church family to support me.

During the summer of 1985 Morfudd began to think that she should be moving into a different type of work, so it was agreed that at the end of the year she would stop travelling with me. One thing about God is that He never lets us get in a rut!

I presumed that I needed to look for a replacement for Morfudd who would do exactly what she had done - but the Lord had other plans! It was the members of our management group who expressed the feeling that God was going to do something new. "Behold I am doing a new thing. Do you perceive it?" I didn't know what it meant or how it applied to us and when, after months of advertising and asking around, no-one suitable could be found to replace Morfudd, I even wondered if I was meant to give up my travelling work.

Tracy Williamson and I got to know each other through Penny, who met her originally when taking a Christian Union meeting at my old school, Chorleywood College.

Tracy, who is partially deaf, was doing a community service volunteer's job at the school in preparation for a course to become a Technical Officer for the blind. The illness she had when young, which caused her deafness, also affected her eyesight, so she has difficulty in lip reading. After she had been at the school for three weeks the headmistress told Tracy that her deafness was a real hindrance to her working with blind people and that perhaps she was looking for the wrong kind of job. Tracy felt devastated by the news because she had been convinced that God had told her she was to work with blind people. As she was unemployed I asked her to help me out until I found a suitable replacement for Morfudd.

Tracy still intended starting the college course the following April and we interviewed several girls who applied for Morfudd's job together. I didn't feel that I could manage concerts without a helper. On the first Sunday of 1986 I was booked to sing at a morning and evening service in Surrey so I asked Tracy to come with Ian and me. As we weren't very organised we nearly left behind the belt of my concert dress, but at the last minute Ian found it. Unfortunately he then left behind the map and the directions to our destination! Somehow we managed to find our way after we had driven around for a while. We certainly missed Morfudd's calm and capable handling of situations like this.

On the way to the church prayer meeting that morning an elderly gentleman pointed out that my dress was caught up at the back! Both Tracy and I were embarrassed - she had checked my make-up, hair and general appearance but neither of us had thought of the need to check me from behind.

During the day I began to realise how much Tracy's deafness cut her off from the activity around her. I knew that she was apprehensive about going into any situation where there were crowds of people because she couldn't follow what was happening. In prayer meetings she found it difficult to participate because people would pray too quietly for her to hear and I longed to be able to communicate to her what was going on. Joining in conversation and hearing what others are saying is obviously an important part of relating to people and because of her deafness Tracy found this difficult. Her situation reminded me of Maureen's.

As my back was painful and I was finding it difficult to concentrate, that night Tracy offered to help me prepare for the service. I take time to listen to God before every performance because each audience has different needs and only He knows how to help them. Although I use similar material each time I need to know which songs will be most suitable and what to say on each occasion.

Since I had started 'on the road' in 1982 I had found I often became spiritually dry and as most of my helpers had been administrators or organisers, the responsibility had been left to me to decide what was right to say and sing. So when Tracy began to look up Bible verses and make suggestions as to what we should do, it was wonderful. I felt a real burden lifting from my shoulders.

She agreed to say something about how Jesus had affected her life and during the concert I sensed the Spirit of God moving in a deep way among the audience as she finished speaking and I sang, "He gives joy to the hopeless, peace to the weary and He binds up the broken hearted," which seemed to embody everything she had been saying. It was inspiring and uplifting and when the minister challenged the congregation to think about what God's love could mean to them about eight people became Christians and twelve other re-dedicated their lives to Christ. Both Tracy and I were staggered and yet thrilled. There had been so many problems and difficulties that day but God had worked in such a wonderful way. The more we worked together the more I began to rely on her contribution to the concerts. Although she couldn't hear *people* well, she did have an ability to listen to the Lord. He often gave her special insights into ways of helping people in the audience who had deep needs. Some would come forward to talk about their problems afterwards and we found it a great privilege to be involved in praying for them and in seeing God touch their lives.

I began to feel that Tracy ought to join the team, but I knew how much the course she was waiting to start meant to her so I didn't mention it, as I didn't want to get in the way of her future plans.

Some time later Tracy said that she wanted to talk to me about something important and it turned out that she had been feeling unsettled about doing her course. She'd had a growing desire to join the team but because of her physical difficulties, had felt unsure about her suitability. She could not imagine, however, any other work which would make her so fulfilled or so happy. When we each realised how the other felt, we were both overjoyed. It was agreed by the management group that Tracy should join the team as a pastoral helper.

Part of the jigsaw still wasn't complete however and we needed an administrator, a driver and also someone to help with the music. We knew that this would mean a big financial commitment but the Lord kept assuring us that it was all part of His plan because He was 'doing a new thing' with and through us. We didn't make it known that we needed more money, either at this time or on later occasions, but the Lord has always provided for us, and increased the amount of gifts we receive when we need it.

When we interviewed Carol Joyce for the administrator's job we knew she was the right person. She is an excellent secretary who is very business-like but also spiritually sensitive. She had been working in an accountant's office and actually took a drop in salary to join us. Carol handles work in the office, but travels on the road with us too and usually takes part in our concerts.

She helps Ian set up the P.A. equipment, organises record sales and makes sure the organisers know what we need. Ruth Valkeith wanted to do a music degree so she gave up working with us at this time and we now have Trudy Wheeler working part-time in the office.

Around this time I also got to know Paul Donnelly. Paul used to be a session rock guitarist. He toured with many groups including the Nolan sisters, but after developing tinnitus and diabetes he found he could not continue in this line of work. His wife Alison became a Christian, then Paul did and the family came to my church. Paul wanted to put his energies into gospel music, so although our musical styles were totally different, we got together at the suggestion of our minister. It was really exciting to find how well we worked together. Paul began to play in some concerts and his sensitive playing enhanced my songs. Alison was a trained singer. She harmonised with me in a lovely way, joining us when the concerts were local and didn't involve leaving their young son David for too long. The combination worked very well and although Paul and Alison are not part of our full-time team we love it when they can travel with us. They add a lot of fun and spiritual depth to our work.

All the team members undertake to help Tracy follow conversations because she obviously can't hear all that is said, especially quick casual remarks. Occasionally we find that none of us have told her about something we have arranged but that doesn't happen often. Fortunately Tracy has a real sense of humour and when there have been misunderstandings, we all have a good laugh together.

With a larger team we outgrew the car and we managed to acquire a van to carry us and our equipment. We had known for some time that we needed a bigger vehicle but we couldn't see how we were going to be able to get this and had made it a matter for much prayer. The Darnalls and their ministry team, who have always shown an interest in our work, were selling the van which had been specifically converted for their use. They let us have it at a reasonable price, for which we were very grateful. Most of the time we travel to concerts in the van together which makes it easier for us all - it's almost like a second home!

Although we are on the road a lot of the time, I do have several hobbies which I find absorbing. Since Muriel taught me the intricacies of cooking I really enjoy getting into the kitchen at home and creating different recipes. I am particularly fond of adding in spices and herbs and when I am abroad I buy cookery books in braille so that I can cook dishes from different countries. Kitchen gadgets are often added to those already filling the cupboards as I find them fascinating and enjoyable to use. A few have to be adapted but most can be used with no difficulty, once somebody has shown me how to work them. Only occasionally have I bought something which has been a waste of money.

I enjoy 'watching' television and sighted people are often surprised that I have a video recorder at home. Sound effects and dialogue give me enough information to be able to follow a programme. Sometimes I can understand a film right through almost to the end only to find that there's hardly any dialogue in the final scene. This is very frustrating!

The interest I developed in radios and tape recorders during my school days has stayed with me. I still love hi-fi equipment, loudspeakers, headphones and anything remotely connected with them. Friends don't always tell me when we walk past hi-fi shops because they know I will be in there ages trying out different items!

When I was teaching at Chorleywood I joined a radio club. Shirley Heskith, who was a part-time teacher, offered to teach anyone who wanted to take the City and Guilds examinations to become a qualified Radio

Amateur. It had always been one of my greatest ambitions to transmit but as I am not electronically minded I didn't know if I would be able to learn about the circuits and mini components which make up radio equipment. I went through the course and Shirley brailled a lot of the material for me. I was the first blind person to go in for the Amateur Radio Exam. Instead of doing a written paper, I was given an oral test. Later on I took the Morse Code Exam and eventually became the first blind lady radio amateur in Britain to be fully licensed.

I was very excited and proceeded to buy a transceiver. Some of my technically minded friends adapted a tuning device so that I could tune my aerial to the different bands and I now have it all set up in my bedroom. Factory owners near my house have kindly agreed to let me have over one hundred feet of aerial wire passing over their roof. Because I live near a railway embankment, reception would be virtually impossible unless I could have a high enough aerial. I am also a CB enthusiast and when people come to visit me, they often comment on the many aerials I have on the roof.

It gave me a real thrill when I was able to talk for the first time to people all over the world who shared my interest. One of the first countries I contacted was Russia. I have a blind friend Graham in London whom I speak to regularly. We make a point of meeting on the air at a pre-arranged time to chat. On other occasions I just go on the air and see who I can contact. "CQ CQ CQ this is G4HGR calling CQ and listening." It's always interesting to see who responds.

# Nineteen

# Always Present

For over a year my back had been giving me a great deal of pain and discomfort. In February 1986 I went into hospital for a few days to have a dye injected into the lumbar fluid, to see if that would show what was causing the problem. The injections gave me a terrific headache and I was glad that Tracy was allowed to stay with me during the day. I was fortunate enough to have a room on my own so she read an exciting book which helped pass some of the time. The tests didn't show anything and by this time I was getting a bit desperate because it was increasingly difficult to walk, sit or stand. Even lying down was painful.

Shortly after this our team went to Cornwall to do some concerts and on the way down I felt God saying to me that I was going to meet someone who could help me - a Christian chiropractor. I didn't feel too happy about this and wondered if I had imagined the whole thing. Anyway I felt that an osteopath would be better than a chiropractor. I asked Sue and Peter Richards, who were my hosts, if they knew of a Christian osteopath. They replied, "No, but we do know a Christian chiropractor called Reg Price and he is coming to your concert".

Sue and Peter knew about my back problem and after praying about it we decided to ring Reg. Even though his surgery was closed, he suggested we go round straightaway and he took several X-rays. I had had X-rays before but nothing had shown up, so I was amazed when the reason for the back pain was found: the sciatic nerve was trapped and two discs had been damaged. Reg gave me several treatments during the fortnight I was in

Cornwall and I certainly felt much better when I returned to Watford.

The next concert tour planned was in Jersey and although I wanted to go very much, I wasn't looking forward to the journey. To make matters worse, the day before we left I tripped over a bucket in the garden and twisted my back. Although I was in agony, I knew that I still had to go to Jersey as I was recording a new LP there. The journey was difficult and during our tour I spent a lot of time lying down. Ian made recordings of the different concerts for the live album. The group *Lovelight*, with whom I had often toured, came with us and sang on the album. This album was different from anything we had done before: it was simple but effective and is called *An Evening with Marilyn Baker*.

My back was still very painful when I returned home. In desperation I phoned Reg Price, who suggested I go back for some more treatment. He invited me to stay with him and his wife Joy for as long as it took me to get back on my feet.

Just before leaving for Cornwall, I had a birthday party at home. I couldn't do anything to help prepare, but Carol Franklin put on some marvellous food and we had a wonderful time. I lay on the camp bed in the lounge and was very touched that so many of my closest friends managed to come.

Tracy and I then headed south and were warmly welcomed by Reg and Joy. All concerts had been cancelled for several weeks and the situation explained to the disappointed organisers. The church in Penzance which Reg and Joy attended held a healing service for me, which I deeply appreciated. Reg told me that more damage had been done by my fall than he had realised and that it would take longer than originally thought for my back to get better. The treatment was very painful and it really was a difficult time for us all. The nights were the worst and Tracy read to me for hours. We found some exciting books and became involved with the characters. Sometimes I was in agony and it was hard to think coherently about anything. Some people say that pain gives endurance - it certainly didn't to me! I think that it is one of the most destructive things human beings have to cope with. Often well-meaning people said or wrote spiritual things like: "You can spend lots of time with the Lord Marilyn now that you can't get about." But it didn't work that way for me - I couldn't even think straight.

I stayed in Cornwall for six weeks and during the last week Carol Franklin stayed with me. By this time there was an improvement and I could go for short slow walks. I was so grateful for that and even now when I wake I say, "Thank You Lord that I can walk".

Even though I was very much better I couldn't stand for long periods and could only walk short distances. My first engagement after the treatment was in Austria and I used a wheelchair. Carol Joyce came with me and pushed the chair when there were no strong men available. I was even pushed to the top of an Austrian mountain! We did have some great fun and the rides at Disneyland were nothing compared to when Denis, a friend of mine, raced me round the streets!

Since then we have done concerts in both this country and abroad. We hope to go to Hong Kong and tour Europe with *Lovelight* in the near future, possibly visiting Poland as well. Wherever we have been though, we receive many lovely letters saying how much records or concerts have helped people through times of personal crisis. It is a tremendous privilege for us to be in a position to do this and the team and I are so grateful to the Lord for His goodness and leading.

Tracy and Carol work well together and complement each other. If I have to go anywhere with only one of them it feels as if something is lacking, almost as if a leg is missing! I know that I need Carol's practical organisational ability, and Tracy's spiritual input makes performing a joy. Concerts are a pleasure and I find it easier to take the opportunities of sharing Jesus' love with the audience now that I feel less spiritually drained.

Tracy and I are also taking a period of three months off from touring to attend Emmanuel Bible College in Birkenhead. When we went for interviews Tracy and I were touched by the friendliness and love shown to us. We are going to college so that we can learn more about the Lord, spending time with Him so that we can communicate His love to others more effectively. During that time Carol will be working at a Bible College in Austria. Being on the road can be taxing and the danger is that we meet so many Christians that we lose touch with the outside world, so it is good to be able to stand back and re-assess what we are doing.

Penny Cooze has left Watford now and although I knew her stay with me was temporary I do miss her. I shall always be grateful both to her and to the Lord for the time she spent with me when I felt so low during and after Mum's illness. We manage to see each other quite often as she doesn't live too far away, which is good for us both. Since she left I don't have anyone living with me long-term. People have been staying for short periods, but it would be great to have someone looking after things at home while I'm away travelling and for this I would need someone permanent.

Sometimes I wish I lived a more settled life or was married and had the same person around me, without all the changes and upheavals every time someone new comes to share my house, but then these changes keep me relying on my heavenly Father. I do feel excited about the future and look forward to it - whatever it holds. Since I moved into my house in Watford I have always relied on Him to protect and help me as He has done so often.

Once when I was on my own and my neighbour was away, I smashed a milk bottle on the kitchen floor. I had

Yuma at the time and was worried in case she would cut herself, so I tried to pick up the pieces myself and got splinters in my fingers. I prayed, "Lord thank You for being here, but I do need some human help now". A few minutes later the door bell rang.

"Is everything alright Marilyn? I felt that I should call in." It was a friend who never called at that time in the morning. She came in and cleared up the mess, explaining that she had been passing the end of my road on the way to work when the Lord had told her to visit me. That is just one example of the many ways that the Lord has shown how much He cares and provides for my needs. Another time a friend for whom I was cooking a meal arrived unexpectedly early - just in time to put out a fire in the frying pan which could have caused a great deal of damage if it had been left another second or two.

Perhaps because of my blindness I have found how very close the Lord wants to come to us and how interested He is in the everyday things in our lives. I know that I am able to depend on Him completely. Being blind is a normal part of my life and I don't see it as suffering in the way some people do. Many of my songs are about God being involved in the details of everyday life and I can sing them confidently knowing from experience that they are true. If I had to make a choice between having a relationship with God or having my sight I would one hundred times over choose the relationship with Him. He has never let me down even though I have let Him down many times.

I believe in the healing power of the Lord and when I was at the Royal College of Music there was a real movement of the Holy Spirit among the students. Many became interested in healing and out of a genuine love for me, wanted me to be healed of my blindness. I was greatly helped by their concern and at that time I firmly believed that the Lord would heal me. I even put a date on when it would happen. On the evening of that day I

went to a healing meeting and waited for the miracle - it
didn't happen. I felt terribly disappointed but despite this
still had an assurance that God hadn't let me down: I had
made a mistake in setting a date because I was trying to
put Him into a corner to make Him do what I wanted.

Some time later when I was teaching in Watford I was
still plagued by the stomach migraine which had caused
me a great deal of discomfort while at Chorleywood
College. One particular evening after school I went to visit
a friend called Nina. She commented on how washed out
I looked and I told her that the stomach pains had been
particularly bad that day.

"Have you prayed about it?" she asked.

"Yes I'm sick of praying about it," was my comment.

"But have you asked the Lord to get to the root of the
problem?" she persisted.

I realised that I hadn't. So after supper we prayed
quietly and Nina tried to sense what the Lord was saying.
I was surprised when she asked if I had ever been in an
oxygen tent. "Yes," I said and she described to me the
picture that God had given her: I had been lying in an
oxygen tent feeling isolated and in need of comforting
arms to hold me. She sensed that as I grew older, I had
experienced that comfort while I was near my parents in
Birmingham, but when I had moved to Chorleywood the
separation had triggered off the feelings of insecurity
again. Nina felt that it was those feelings that lay at the
root of my stomach pains. As she talked to me, I realised
that the pains had only come when I was at school - never
when I was at home on holiday. Somehow I knew that
what Nina said was true: although I hadn't been aware of
it, now that I was living in Watford I was still missing my
parents.

She prayed that God would go back with me to the
time when I was a baby and that He would come close to
me while I was in the oxygen tent and put His arms
around me. I felt peaceful and the next morning I had a

feeling of a deep security and well-being which I hadn't experienced before. Since then I have only ever experienced a slight twinge of pain when I have been over-anxious or under real pressure. This was my first experience of God healing my emotions and setting me free from experiences of the past.

A short while after this I felt that God was going to heal my blindness as well, so I went forward at a crusade healing service. Several people laid hands on me and prayed. I was then told not to open my eyes until I believed that I could see. My immediate reaction was to panic. Not being able to remember having had any vision I just couldn't conceive what it was like to see!

When I didn't receive my sight I felt devastated. It affected my Christian life badly: if I had heard God wrongly about this incident, then how could I be sure I would hear Him correctly about other things? Deep in my heart I felt let down by God and I found it very difficult to pray. The whole question of healing now made me feel cynical.

This happened the year before my first trip to Canada with Carol Franklin. While on that holiday we went to a Christian Holiday Camp and I had a talk with one of the speakers. He was a very fatherly type of person and although he didn't say a great deal to me he understood how these experiences had knocked my faith. He felt that some of the people who had prayed for my healing had been unwise so he prayed with me, asking God to heal the disappointments in my heart. Although I didn't feel anything at the time, afterwards it was as if new seeds of trust were planted. God's love had not failed me and I began to build up my relationship with the Lord again. Now when I come across the new move of the Spirit with the *Signs and Wonders Seminars,* I don't feel disappointed, but I welcome what God is doing. I do feel though that people must be careful when they pray for healing with someone because it is tremendously important that the person does not feel condemned or blamed in any way if there is no visible improvement. After the prayer time the person should feel strengthened in his or her faith whatever happens. It is often alleged that people aren't healed because they lack faith but it is possible to become so faith-centred that Jesus, the Person in whom we should have faith, is forgotten.

Faith cannot be worked up by an individual: it is something which God plants within a heart and I believe that when we are ill or have needs, we must bring them to our loving Heavenly Father knowing that we can trust Him totally for the outcome. In the Bible it says that 'God did not spare His only Son, but freely gave Him up for us'. If God was prepared to do this much for us then we know that He will freely give us everything else. God knows what is best for us and it is not necessarily what we want. We have no need to be anxious, because we can rest in His wisdom.

I still miss my Mum a great deal and think of her often. We used to 'phone each other regularly and chat about all kinds of things. Trivial or serious, it didn't matter: we were good friends who loved to share thoughts and ideas. I knew she cared for me and was concerned about how I was. Mum played a special role in my life which can never be filled by anyone else but I still have my Dad and a caring church family who help me in many ways. I also know the care of God and my greatest desire is to communicate His love to others. It seems that God has given me music as a vehicle for doing this and I shall carry on writing songs as long as He inspires me to do so. My natural gift is not in writing poetry but as long as I have God's inspiration I shall carry on. I can't write a song about anything unless it speaks powerfully to me and has affected my life.

The melody and words for the first line of the song *Jesus You are Changing Me* came into my head as I was walking down Watford High Street with Yuma. I'd been feeling spiritually low at the time and I thought, "I am not going to write a song like that, because I don't feel as if I am being changed". But then I recalled verse 18 of 2 Corinthians chapter 3 which says that we are being changed from one degree of glory to another. The Lord seemed to say to me, "Do you believe My Word or not?"

The following weekend I went to stay at Torch House and felt especially cared for by my friends there. When I returned to Watford I felt the Lord say, "I love you even more than your friends at Torch House do and I am committed to changing you. As long as you allow Me to work in your life I can do it. Nothing is too difficult for Me." Then as the truth of what I was learning began to flood my heart, the remainder of the lyrics came together.

Many people say that my songs speak to them because the words express how they feel and think. I am glad about that because I am an ordinary person with ordinary feelings and I just want to share what I have found in Jesus. I have an 'artistic temperament' which means that I am up and down at times, but I am growing more secure in God's love and my moods are becoming less changeable. Those who live with me or know me well realise that I am neither a super saint nor an angel! I love a good laugh and I hate being treated like a piece of precious china. I try to express my true feelings and thoughts when I write songs because I don't see any value in not being honest. But songs with no answers, with the ending left in the air, annoy me. I want to be positive and point people to Jesus, Who is the answer to all the needs and emptiness in people's lives today. The deep joy which Jesus gives is something that no-one can take away and we can experience it no matter what our circumstances.

He gives joy to the hopeless
Peace to the weary
And He binds up the broken hearted.
Did you know that Jesus wants to be your greatest

friend?
He knows all about you and His love for you cannot
end.
He made you for a purpose, He's interested in you
So give Him a chance and let His love shine
through.

# MARILYN BAKER DISCOGRAPHY

*Albums and cassettes*
*He Gives Joy* Pilgrim PLM 455 PC 455
*Whispers of God* Pilgrim PLM 488 PC 488
*Refresh me Lord* Pilgrim PLM 495 PC 495
*Marilyn Baker* Word WSTR 9670 WSTC 9670
*An Evening With Marilyn Baker* Word WRDR 3028
WRDC 3028
*Rest in His Love* Pilgrim PLM 534 PC 534
*Close to His Heart* Word WSTR 9688 WSTC 9688

*Video*
*Marilyn Baker Songwriter* CTVC Film Library

*Songbook*
*Rest in My Love* Word 9514

# THE CROSS AND THE SWASTIKA
## F T Grossmith

What finally happened to Hitler's men? Based on his research into military records and his correspondence with survivors of those involved, the author has written a fascinating account of their last months in Nuremberg.

THE CROSS AND THE SWASTIKA discloses the amazing impact of an unknown US army chaplain, Major Henry Gerecke, on the lives of the most hated men of the age. Dealing with men like Hess and Göring, his task was no easy one, but he saw several of his 'congregation' come to Christ before he accompanied them to the gallows.

"… one of the most remarkable testimonies to the all encompassing grace of God I have ever read"   "… a book that is compelling"

ON BEING, AUSTRALIA

"Plenty of surprises … gripping story"

EVANGELISM TODAY

"Classic documentary and a most moving piece of writing"

BAPTIST TIMES

"One of the most thrilling books read for years"

WESTERN GAZETTE, YEOVIL

Born in Birkenhead and brought up in Anfield, Liverpool, F T Grossmith has engaged in evangelistic work and convention speaking in Britian and Europe. He has been featured many times in radio and television programmes, and is married with four daughters.

Catalogue Number YB 9152                    £2.00

# HOW TO HELP YOUR CHILD SAY "NO" TO SEXUAL PRESSURE
**Josh McDowell**

Whether your children are 7 or 19 they face tremendous pressure in today's permissive society. In HOW TO HELP YOUR CHILD SAY NO TO SEXUAL PRESSURE you will:

* Learn why your children feel such immense pressure to be sexually active.

* Examine how the media distorts their views on love and sex.

* Discover when to share the reasons to wait.

Josh McDowell equips you with practical "how to say no" principles for parents of teenagers, as well as creative preventative measures for parents of preteens. This realistic and sensitive, yet compelling book will help you instill within your children that waiting until marriage is the best choice they can make about sex.

Josh McDowell has been a travelling representative for Campus Crusade for Christ for over twenty years. A graduate of Wheaton College and Talbot Theological Seminary, he is author of eighteen best-selling books in the USA. He is resident instructor at The Julian Centre, San Diego, USA.

Catalogue Number YB 9150          £2.50

# LIVING ON THE DEVIL'S DOORSTEP
## Floyd McClung

Just an ordinary young couple from American suburbia - but they dared to dream they could make a difference.

Their dream took them all over the world: first to the backstreets of Kabul, Afghanistan and later to the bright lights of Amsterdam's Red Light District.

Share in their adventures, their heartaches and their joys as they reach out to people in need - sharing their home with hippies in Kabul or working amongst addicts, prostitutes and Aids victims in Amsterdam.

With their two children, Floyd and Sally McClung still live 'on the Devil's Doorstep' where God is at work bringing hope to hopeless people.

Their story will speak to all those who want help and inspiration for their lives.

Catalogue Number YB 9142          £2.95